In the
LIGHT
of the
GOSPEL

In the
LIGHT
of the
GOSPEL

Short Meditations

FERNANDO OCÁRIZ

Scepter

Published by Scepter Publishers, Inc.
info@scepterpublishers.org
www.scepterpublishers.org
800-322-8773
New York

Text by Studio Red Design
Cover by Rose Design
Cover Image: Armenian Christian illustrated manuscript showing the four Evangelists, 14th century. Alamy.com

Library of Congress Control Number:
2020947003

ISBN: 978-1-59417-413-1

Printed in the United States of America

Contents

Introduction 1

1. There is Nothing Stronger than Love 3

2. God Keeps On Calling 4

3. Saying Yes Always 5

4. Mother of Hope 6

5. Families that Spread Light 8

6. Between the Two of Us 9

7. Mary, God's Joy 10

8. Silence 12

9. A Hidden God 13

10. Gratitude 14

11. Peace to All Mankind 15

12. Making Ourselves Little 16

13. Breathing the Gospel 17

14. Love Never Retires 18

15. Into Egypt 19

16. Listening: Silence in Action 20

17. God's Children in the Church 22

18. Youth and Vocation 23

19. Going Forth 25

20. Mary as Friend 27

21. "Melting" Into God 29

22. Citizens of Heaven 30

23. God in My House 31

24. Lovable Duty...32

25. Freedom of Spirit 34

26. Signs of Thirst...35

27. Going Out to Meet Our Contemporaries....................36

28. Old Boat, New Boat...37

29. Young at Heart: Facing Forward................................38

30. Discernment in Love 39

31. Their Home, Their Task, Their Native Land...............40

32. Joy..41

33. The Actions of God's Children...................................43

34. The Secret of Youth... 44

35. Horizons...45

36. Compassion: Empathy in Suffering 47

37. Openness.. 48

38. Understanding 49

39. Discrepancy...50

40. Good Soil 51

41. Putting God First..52

42. Abandonment in God...53

43. Seeing 54

44. Joy without Fear 55

45. Nourishment...56

46. Under the Same Roof...57

47. Doing Our Own Work..58

48. Cooperators with Christ...60

49. Center and Root 61

50. Malicious Gossip Normalized..62

51. With Your Help 63

52. Jesus' Promise..64

53. The Present Transfigured...65

54. Without Him We Can Do Nothing.......................................66

55. Faith in Mercy 67

56. Lukewarmness..68

57. Good Friends with Everyone 69

58. Living Stones 70

59. Jesus' Freedom 71

60. What Do They Need? 73

61. Souls of Prayer 74

62. Wretchedness and Greatness..75

63. Conversion..76

64. The Eternal Feast Day..77

65. A Great Feast 78

66. Adopted and Raised Up 79

67. Our Way of Praying..80

68. They Went Up to the Temple 81

69. The Last Place 82

70. Questions for Young People 84

71. Taking a Risk...86

72. The Good of God 87

73. The Good of Our Neighbor 88

74. Patience and Impatience...89

75. Everyone's Brothers and Sisters.....................................90

76. Love Steps Forward.. 91

77. To the End...93

78. Being Loved by God...95

79. True Concern..96

80. Clothed in Christ...97

81. From Mass to Mass 98

82. He Calls the Poor..99

83. Image of God 100

84. Our Life 101

85. Peace and Uncertainty 102

86. Transmitting Peace...104

87. Uncomplicated..105

88. No Distinctions 106

89. Innovating Love 107

90. What We Find Hard 108

91. The Joy of God's Children...109

92. Newness 110

93. Apostolate with Soul...111

94. The World Will Hate You 112

95. Sensing Your Presence...114

96. Communion of Love 115

97. Unity and Division..116

98. The Center of Our Hopes 117

99. Suffering with Jesus 118

100. Tiredness in Prayer...120

101. Seeing with Christ's Eyes..121

102. Pluralism and Charity 122

103. King 124

104. Ecce Homo: A Vulnerable God 126

105. Filling the World with Kindness 128

106. Cross and Paradise 129

107. Suffering and Clarity 130

108. Children with Mary and Joseph 131

109. Christ's Availability 133

110. Consoling Christ and His Mother 134

111. Christ in Other People 136

112. A New Light 137

113. There You Will See Him 138

114. A Question from Our Lord 139

115. Despoiled 140

116. The Promise of the Spirit 141

117. The Ultimate Reason 143

118. Communion and Eternity 144

119. Vessels of Clay 145

Index 146

Introduction

"No man ever spoke like this man!" (Jn 7:46)

Today, in very different parts of the world, millions of people are meditating on, listening to, reading, and praying about the Gospel. Jesus' life and preaching were the start of a conversation with the women and men of all times. "Jesus is ready to speak to everyone. And his words heal, console, and enlighten."[1]

This book is a collection of short pieces starting off from, and sometimes dialoguing with, a verse from the New Testament, almost always the Gospels.

In the Light of the Gospel originated in some of the preaching notes I made from 1977 onwards. As such, the pieces are neither exhaustive nor exegetical. Now, at the publisher's request, I have put them into publishable shape, but they still have the schematic style of the original notes. The current book also includes other more recent notes used for various letters and pastoral messages.[2]

The pieces have different dates and different subjects, generally following the order of Jesus Christ's life and teachings, starting off from the Gospel quote selected (sometimes in retrospect) to head the passage. A few are headed by quotes from other New Testament books, and in these cases, rather than the chronological sequence, they are connected in some way with the topic of the preceding piece.

The purpose of this book, like the notes it originated from,

---

1. St. Josemaría, Letter dated 24 October 1965, 10.
2. Some notes from 1992 were afterwards published, with slight modifications, in the booklet *God as Father in the Message of Blessed Josemaría Escrivá*, Scepter, Princeton NJ, 1994.

is to help people to pray and invite them to enter into more direct contact with Jesus Christ, who is the light of our lives, and who arouses different aspirations in each person at different times.

In the Gospel, Word and Truth come together and offer a window onto heaven. "The Word was with God" (Jn 1:1), and when the fullness of time came, the Word became man and passed on to us the truth about God and the world. God revealed himself to us as Love. In direct contact with the Gospel we find Christ in his sacred humanity, and if we let him, he dwells in the center of our lives.

Getting to know Jesus is a personal experience, but not a solitary one. Together with Our Lord, we get acquainted with the people who met him during his life here on earth and who were transformed by their relationship with him. As we come closer to Christ we also meet our neighbors, living with us in this present world, the sisters and brothers whom Jesus Christ seeks out in love; he talks to everyone.

May this book renew our desire to meditate on the Gospel with a contemplative, listening attitude. From time to time we will recognize the Teacher's voice more clearly, maybe asking us for a response. Then, with God's help, may we be able to say to him, like Our Lady, "let it be to me according to your word" (Lk 1:38).

Fernando Ocáriz
Rome, May 31, 2020,
during the Covid-19 lockdown.

1. There is Nothing Stronger than Love

March 24, 1977

"We know and believe the love God has for us" (1 Jn 4:16).

It is not difficult, with grace and faith, to believe in general terms that God loves us; and we can list many gifts we have received from his hands.

But in practice, our faith in his love often is not something we actually live by. Because if he loves us all the time—when we are overwhelmed, tired, in difficulties, keenly experiencing our own wretchedness, even when we are sinful—if he loves us in spite of all this and with all this, why do we worry? Why do we lose patience?

If we really believe that God loves us, if we believe in the love he has for us, what more do we want? What more could we need?

So in the silence of our prayer, in God's presence, under his merciful gaze, it is right for us to consider the gifts he grants us, starting with the one that underlies all the rest: his love and faithfulness toward each of us.

And when difficulties come, or injustice, or a situation where we lose the peace and joy that come from abandoning ourselves in Jesus Christ, let us turn back to him with faith, saying like the apostles: *Domine, adauge nobis fidem!* — "Lord, increase our faith . . . in the love you have for us" (Lk 17:5).

Then we'll be able to experience for ourselves the meaning of St. Paul's confident exclamation: "If God is for us, who is against us?" (Rom 8:31). There is nothing and nobody on earth stronger than the love God has for each of us.

2. God Keeps On Calling

February 12, 2020

"How shall I know this? For I am an old man, and my wife is advanced in years" (Lk 1:18).

Elizabeth and Zachary had no children and had given up hope of having any. The passing of time must have seemed like long lines of possibilities that vanished successively into nothing.

So many elderly people today maybe see themselves as useless, in a world where doing counts for more than being. And in the times of Elizabeth and Zachary too, social attitudes were not favorable; their childlessness weighed heavily upon them.

How could Elizabeth and Zachary suspect that they, at their age, had been chosen to play an important role in the plan of redemption? Their son, John, was to be Christ's forerunner.

Jesus incarnated the natural rhythms of human life: infancy, adolescence, and maturity. And in a sense, his physical and mental sufferings cast light on old age too.

The whole of Jesus' life was redemptive, and he fulfilled the highest point of his mission at the gates of death and through his death itself. He made us into God's children, he gave us the Eucharist and the New Commandment, he promised us the Holy Spirit, and he gave us his Mother.

Old age is as good a time as any other to respond when the shepherd whistles his summons. God keeps on calling us to give ourselves in service to others and grants us the vigor of youth on the inside.

3. Saying Yes Always

March 6, 1979

"And Mary said, 'Behold, I am the handmaid of the Lord; let it be to me according to your word'" (Lk 1:38).

Mary's "yes" to the angel, in her home in Nazareth, opens the doors to the Incarnation and Redemption. Her consent changes the course of history.

As we don't lack God's grace, we too can say "yes" to the calls Our Lord makes to us throughout the day, even though it will normally be in things of slight importance.

But it can often happen that we don't recognize something we see or hear at a given moment as a call from God—a request for help, a change of plans, the intimation that we could be more generous in this or that situation.

Sometimes we fail to see or hear those calls because we don't want to. At other times our senses are dulled by exterior or interior noise. Then, like the blind man Bartimaeus, let's beg, "Master, let me receive my sight" (Mk 10:51). And we can add, "Lord, may I want to see you; may I listen to you, may I want to listen to you . . ." so that, hundreds of times a day, we can repeat Mary's powerful words of assent: "Let it be to me according to your word."

4. Mother of Hope

May 5, 2020

". . . a virgin betrothed to a man whose name was Joseph, of the house of David; and the virgin's name was Mary" (Lk 1:27).

She replied to the angel's announcement: "Behold, I am the handmaid of the Lord . . ." (Lk 1:38). And the Word was made flesh.

For any mother, expecting a son or daughter is a time of human hopes. In Mary that hope must also have had a universal dimension, a salvific dimension, because she knew she was carrying the world's Redeemer in her womb. Her gaze, as she looked forward to the future, somehow included each of us. From the time of her pregnancy onwards, Our Lady must have felt the weight of the whole of mankind, of being the "New Eve."

Mary's fullness of grace did not exempt her from suffering; it was present in her life from Bethlehem to Calvary. Pope Francis says that Mary "teaches us the virtue of waiting, even when everything appears nonsensical . . . , even when God seems to be eclipsed by the evil in the world." She sustains us along our way, telling us to "'Rise! Look ahead, look at the horizon,' because she is Mother of Hope."[3]

In the light of faith, suffering takes on meaning, becomes more bearable, and can even end up by becoming a locus of clarity, peace, and inner joy.

We don't want anyone to suffer, and at the same time, because we know that suffering is part of human life, we learn to bear it with other people, to wrap it in love. In Benedict XVI's encyclical *Spe salvi* we read: "It is not by sidestepping or fleeing from suffering that we are healed, but rather by our capacity

3.   Pope Francis, General Audience, May 10, 2017.

for accepting it, maturing through it, and finding meaning through union with Christ, who suffered with infinite love."[4]

To the Blessed Virgin Mary, Mother of Hope, we especially commend the present and future of the Church. Her firm trust in her Son kept the nascent Church united in a time of weakness: several disciples fled, one had denied Jesus, others doubted, and all of them were scared. She infused hope (see Acts 1:14).

4. Pope Benedict XVI, *Spe salvi*, 37.

5. Families that Spread Light

September 1, 2018

"An angel of the Lord appeared to him in a dream, saying, 'Joseph, son of David, do not fear to take Mary your wife, for that which is conceived in her is of the Holy Spirit'" (Mt 1:20).

An angel restored St. Joseph's peace of mind when he was dismayed.

The story of the home at Nazareth was "no idealized fairy tale." The Holy Family was undoubtedly the happiest that there ever has been or ever will be on earth, but they still had to face up to difficulties and serious problems right from the start.

"God works for good with those who love him" (Rom 8:28), wrote St. Paul. Many of us will remember how St. Josemaría summarized this in just three words: *Omnia in bonum*, "everything is for the good" (Furrow, 127).

Everything is for the good: money problems that force a change of plan; the challenges of raising the children; the difficulties of combining a demanding job with taking care of the house . . . Everything is for the good, if we place everything in God's hands. He will give us the strength to turn setbacks into opportunities to grow as a family, to make those crises, great or small, bring the family closer together, because everyone pulls together to bear them with love.

Amidst its imperfections and difficulties, each family is a civilizing influence and a source of good when they make the effort to foster communion, forgiveness and solidarity. They don't need to wait until everything in their own home is functioning perfectly. Every family can give light and warmth to other families, friends, neighbors, and more.

6. Between the Two of Us

March 5, 2014

"Behold, a virgin shall conceive and bear a son, and his name shall be called Emmanuel (which means, God with us)." (Mt 1:23).

Christ stays with us.

Sometimes, before starting on a piece of work, St. Josemaría would say to Our Lord, "Jesus, let's do this between the two of us."

Jesus is with us, and we are his instruments. This requires us to behave well and work well; otherwise we would in some way be leaving Our Lord in a bad light, by being bad instruments of his.

Jesus and I. It is a relationship that is personal, unique, and irreplaceable.

But, at the same time, union with Christ, if it is real, becomes a union with the Body of Christ that is the Church: communion with God, the communion of the saints.

The relationship "Jesus and I" becomes a union for others and with others.

7. Mary, God's Joy

May 31, 1999

"Blessed is she who believed" (Lk 1:45).

Mary goes to meet Elizabeth; who else could understand her better? They talk about the sons they are expecting, Jesus and John. The scene of the Visitation is flooded with the Holy Spirit (Lk 1:39). John recognizes the presence of God and exults with joy, already acting as the forerunner. Announcing Christ means having and giving true happiness.

Elizabeth praises Mary's faith, and Mary proclaims the Magnificat (Lk 1:46–56): "My soul magnifies the Lord . . ." Understanding the Greek word for "magnify" as meaning "make great," we want to glorify God, give him glory by "making him great" in our soul and in our deeds; by opening up the whole space of our life to him. And by making great—by loving and serving—other people.

In this hymn Mary recalls the promise of God's mercy "from generation to generation," and God's preferential love for the humble. Mary relies on her great faith in God whenever she doesn't understand—"Son, why have you treated us so?" (Lk 2:48)—especially at the foot of the Cross. By that time, John had been beheaded by Herod; at the foot of the Cross her memories of the Visitation must have seemed clouded with sorrow, but her faith and her hope in Christ's Resurrection remained clear.

Mary, before and more than anyone else, fulfilled the aspiration later expressed by St. Paul: "Now I rejoice in my sufferings for your sake, and in my flesh I complete what is lacking in Christ's afflictions for the sake of his body, that is, the church" (Col 1:24).

The shining faith of Mary and Elizabeth, as they contemplated God's greatness, form a painful contrast with the contemporary pessimism which often sees God as a barrier to human fulfilment. May we reflect in our lives the joy and freedom born of knowing through faith that God has made us his children. Children, not slaves (see Gal 4:7).

8. Silence

December 16, 2019

"And she gave birth to her first-born son and wrapped him in swaddling cloths, and laid him in a manger" (Lk 2:7).

In the silence of Bethlehem, hand in hand with Mary and Joseph, our joys, our hopes, and our sorrows find their place, with renewed clarity.

On the night when we celebrate the birth of the Child Jesus, even external things echo our inner attitude. In the silence of the night, God's Son is waiting for us.

Let us draw close to the simplicity and silence of Bethlehem! Let us allow ourselves to be wrapped in the recollection of the heart that is "like the doorkeeper of the interior life."[5]

---

5. St. Josemaría, *The Way*, 281.

9. A Hidden God

August 21, 1980

"And this will be a sign for you: you will find a babe wrapped in swaddling cloths and lying in a manger" (Lk 2:12).

Even when Jesus was born, an angel had to give precise directions to the shepherds: wrapped in swaddling cloths, and lying in a manger. Without those details they would not have been able to recognize the baby as the Messiah, the Savior.

Why doesn't he show himself openly to the whole world? Why doesn't he show himself to us more clearly, today, in our homes, in our towns, in our workplaces?

There is only one answer: his love, because "God is love" (1 Jn 4:8).

If God showed himself more obviously than he actually does, the sin of those who refuse to recognize him would be all the greater; hidden as he is, he offers his grace to everyone. We could consider the fact that a manifestation of God in his power and majesty, here and now, would not lead to the salvation of more souls, but to an increase in the gravity of our sins and our lack of generosity.

The same happens with the Risen Christ. To see that this is so, we only have to look at the Pharisees who did not believe in him even though they had seen his miracles. Even then, Jesus chose the path of not being evident, of not making himself manifest to everyone.

Lord, "truly, you are a God who hide yourself" (Is 45:15[6]): hidden out of love. Hidden, but not invisible (see Jn 1:1–18).

---

6. RSV-2CE translation.

10. Gratitude

March 8, 2001

"Glory to God in the highest" (Lk 2:14).

Thank you, Lord! Because we exist, because you created us, because you maintain us in being.

Thank you, Lord, for your grace, your forgiveness, your providence; thank you for making us your children.

Thank you, Lord, for our baptismal calling, for the way you have led us by the hand, in spite of our poor response.

Thank you, Lord, for the trust and confidence you have in us, which we did not and do not deserve.

Lord, forgive our ingratitude—for all the times when we haven't thanked you!

May we never forget the reason we should be constantly grateful: God's love for us. God, in Christ, became one of us and guides our steps.

First of all, I should think of what God has done and does for me. I shouldn't try to base my security on what I have done and do for God, because what is mine will always be too little, and whatever I do will, in reality, be itself a gift from God.

Ut in gratiarum semper actione maneamus! May we persevere in constant thanksgiving!

11. Peace to All Mankind

December 19, 2018

" … on earth peace among men with whom he is pleased!" (Lk 2:14).

The angels' song echoes throughout the world, stirring up in us a joyous hope; above all, because peace has drawn close to us and we can contemplate it in the face of a Child. "He is our peace" (Eph 2:14), St. Paul later wrote as he reflected on the mystery of Jesus Christ.

The world stands in great need of peace. Each of us, our families, the place where we work, the environment around us, need this Child whom the angels announce as the Savior (see Lk 2:11).

Without him, every effort to bring peace to hearts will fall short. Therefore the Church never ceases speaking about Jesus to mankind, like the shepherds after seeing him in the manger (see Lk 2:16–18). We too want to make him known to others. In apostolic work "it is Christ we should talk about, not ourselves."[7]

Let's often meditate on the great mystery of God's love in this Child who is born to us (see Is 9:5). How easy it is to find or regain peace and serenity as we contemplate the scene of the Nativity, letting ourselves be captivated by Jesus in the manger, with Mary and Joseph on either side! As we contemplate this mystery of love, Our Lord will also give us new zest to pass it on to others.

---

7. St. Josemaría, *Christ Is Passing By*, 163.

12. Making Ourselves Little

December 29, 2019

"And [the shepherds] went with haste, and found Mary and Joseph, and the babe lying in a manger" (Lk 2:16).

Looking at Jesus in the manger, wrapped about with the immense love of Mary and Joseph, we want to feel like him: little. Contemplating the Child Jesus, we hear echoes of Isaiah's prophecy: "God made his Word short, he abbreviated it" (Is 10:23, cited by Benedict XVI, homily, December 24, 2006), which is also mentioned by St. Paul (see Rom 9:28). God, in Christ, has become little for us.

We too want to make ourselves little, especially before you, Lord: to have the trust and simplicity of small children. And we also want to make ourselves little before other people: to see ourselves as less important, with zeal for service, dedication, genuine interest in their needs, and without being oversensitive. We want people to be able to rely on us.

To do that, like the shepherds, we need to go quickly, filled with peace and longing to find the Savior, not stopping on the way.

What stops us from going quickly to Our Lord? It can happen that we lose sight of our goal. We are coming to find you, Jesus. Yet sometimes we lose our way, and we fail to find you in our work—especially when it is difficult—in our relaxation, in our family life, in other people.

At such moments, let's look at this Child who is God and who chooses to submit to the law of normality and suffering, from the manger in Bethlehem onwards.

13. Breathing the Gospel

April 5, 2017

"Mary kept all these things, pondering them in her heart" (Lk 2:19).

Reading the Gospel with love helps us to grow in friendship with Jesus. As we contemplate Our Lord's life, God will surprise us with new lights.

Although we may sometimes think that our Gospel reading isn't making any impression on us, later on there will come to our lips or thoughts Jesus' words, his reactions, his gestures, which light up the ordinary or not so ordinary situations of our lives. What we need to do is breathe the Gospel, the Word of God.

If we really have that keen desire to get deep inside the Gospel, when we talk about Christian living to our friends we will be able to pass on the great news of God's love for each and every person more radiantly.

St. Ambrose said, "Gather the water of Christ . . . . Fill then the bosom of your mind, that your ground may be moistened . . . and once filled, water others."[8]

May Our Lady teach us to keep and ponder in our heart, as she did, everything concerning Jesus, so that we can travel, and help others to travel, along paths of contemplation; each of us where God is calling us.

8. St. Ambrose, *Letter 2*, 4.

14. Love Never Retires

February 12, 2020

"Now there was a man in Jerusalem, whose name was Simeon…. And inspired by the Spirit he came into the temple" (Lk 2:25, 27).

It was two elderly people, Anna and Simeon, as well as the angels and shepherds, who proclaimed the Savior's birth to the world.

On one of his birthdays St. Josemaría noted that he was "always beginning," because "years bestow neither wisdom nor holiness." As time passes, Jesus wants us to continue growing, because our goal is identification with him.

The elderly are a force, an asset for the Church and society. With their human witness, the memory of their lives and their long experience of a personal relationship with God, they are "living stones," foundations to support the new generations who sometimes lack accessible role models.

St. Paul advised Titus, "Bid the older men be temperate, serious, sensible, sound in faith, in love, and in steadfastness" (Ti 2:2).

In daily life, older people communicate by what they do, rather than in words; by humbly letting themselves be cared for in their limitations and sicknesses, by smiling when in pain, by not complaining, by thanking people for acts of service, and by offering other acts of service themselves, not hiding the fact that they pray and trust in God. The sight of an older person saying the Rosary alone is something that may remain in someone's heart for life. They teach us that love knows nothing of retirement.

December 29, 2019

"Rise, take the child and his mother, and flee to Egypt, and remain there till I tell you; for Herod is about to search for the child, to destroy him" (Mt 2:13).

A major disruption occurs: God has to flee in haste, because people want to kill him. St. Joseph organizes everything and sets off straight away, by night, not even waiting till it is light, and not knowing whether they are going to be away for weeks, months, or years.

We can imagine how worried Our Lady and St. Joseph must have been as they began their journey, but they went without protest, with the inner joy of doing God's will and the certainty that he was with them.

Let us ask St. Joseph to help us be prompt to take up God's suggestions, even though sometimes, for a short while, they may seem meaningless or disrupt our plans.

We want to imitate the Holy Family and set off in a new direction: a new job, a new situation, a new person to help.

Faith will move us to set off into the Egypt of what we are not expecting.

16. Listening: Silence in Action

February 20, 2020

"They found him in the temple, sitting among the teachers, listening to them and asking them questions" (Lk 2:46).

The Word speaks, but he also keeps silent and listens, like a newborn baby.

As he did in the temple, there are many more episodes where Jesus again keeps silent and listens: when he writes on the ground while being questioned by those who wish to stone the sinful woman (Jn 8:6); on the mountain when he prays in silence to his Father (Lk 6:12); when he is nailed to the Cross (Jn 19:18) . . . And also today, in the Eucharist, Jesus continues to listen to our words.

Prayer is a school of silence, listening, and action. Jesus asks us, like Peter, "Do you love me?" (Jn 21:16).

The condition for any dialogue, beyond the actual words used, is to love, to respect, to pay attention, and to put ourselves in the other person's place. There is dialogue in the affectionate exchange of glances between a woman and a man whose love continues to grow in their old age. In the caress given by a father to his sick daughter. In the tears that say sorry and ask for forgiveness. In listening when someone needs to talk, or when we are corrected, or when someone suggests an area in which we could improve.

The walls that prevent us from listening are usually pride, self-importance, the arrogance of poorly understood authority, and the selfishness that blocks our ears to the needs of a family member, a friend, or a neighbor. Superficiality and haste: not noticing, not being on the same wavelength, not realizing. It is disheartening for people to feel they are not being listened to by someone who ought to listen to them.

May God grant us the gift of listening, of escaping from our selfish monologue, and learning to have a genuine feeling for other people, meaning that we can share in what they are living through, in what is happening to them.

17. God's Children in the Church

March 1, 1992

"I have baptized you with water; but he will baptize you with the Holy Spirit" (Mk 1:8).

Through baptism we are born to Christian life from the Church and in the Church. Our supernatural life always grows *in Ecclesia*—in the Church.

Therefore our birth as God's children is *ex Deo*, from God, but also *ex Ecclesia*, from the Church. We are children of God insofar as we are children of the Church and vice versa; the one presupposes and includes the other.

The motherhood of the Church is in a way an expression or manifestation of the fatherhood of God toward his adopted children.

The fact that we are children of God and children of the Church has, by God's design, its continuation in the fact that as Christians we are necessarily children of the Pope, who is truly "father and teacher."

18. Youth and Vocation

September 18, 2018

"The two disciples heard him say this, and they followed Jesus" (Jn 1:37).

To fulfil God's plans in our own lives, to follow our specific vocation, we need not only light to see the path, but also the strength to want to follow him.

When he asks for something, he is in fact offering us a gift. It's not we who are doing him a favor; it is God who lights up our lives, filling them with meaning.

If only young people and adults alike understood that holiness is not only no obstacle to our own dreams, but is in fact their culmination! Our desires, projects, and loves can all be part of God's plans.

Christian life does not lead us to identify ourselves with an idea but with a person: Jesus Christ. If faith is to light our steps, as well as asking ourselves "What is Jesus Christ to me?" we need to think "What am I to Jesus Christ?"

We will then discover the gifts that Our Lord has given us, which are directly connected with our own mission. In this way, there will mature in us, progressively, an inner attitude of openness to other people's needs. We'll learn to place ourselves at the service of everyone, and we will see more clearly the place God has entrusted to us in this world.

In a society of people who tend to think far too much about material well-being, faith helps us to raise our eyes and discover the true dimensions of our own lives.

If we are bearers of the Gospel, our journey through this world will bear fruit. The whole of society will unquestionably benefit from a generation of young people who ask themselves, based on faith in God's love for us: "What is my mission in this life? What kind of mark will I leave behind?"

19. Going Forth

February 14, 2017

"Philip found Nathanael, and said to him, 'We have found him of whom Moses in the law and also the prophets wrote, Jesus of Nazareth'" (Jn 1:45).

Bringing the joy of the Gospel to many souls will enable them to feel the attractiveness of Jesus Christ.

This "going forth," this dynamism that God wants to stir up in believers, is not a strategy but the strength of the Holy Spirit, Uncreated Love.

"In a Christian, in a child of God, friendship and charity are one and the same thing. They are a divine light which spreads warmth."[9]

The ideal of love of God leads us to make friends with many people. We Christians don't "do apostolic work," we are apostles! That is what constitutes the "Church going forth" that Pope Francis talks about.[10]

The current situation of evangelization makes it more necessary than ever for us to give priority to personal contact. This relational aspect is at the heart of the spirit of doing apostolic work that St. Josemaría found in the Gospel narratives.

In this personal apostolate, let's not forget the enlightening power of our example. St. Paul VI famously said, "Modern man listens more willingly to witnesses than to teachers; and," he added, "if he does listen to teachers, it is because they are witnesses."[11]

9.   St. Josemaría, *The Forge*, 565.
10. Pope Francis, *Evangelii Gaudium*, 20.
11. St. Paul VI, *Evangelii Nuntiandi*, 41.

Let us pray that in our contemporary culture, in today's world, there may be plenty of approachable faces—friends—who pass on Jesus' message with real credibility.

20. Mary as Friend

May 15, 2020

"When the wine failed, the mother of Jesus said to him, 'They have no wine'" (Jn 2:3).

Our Lady inspires us with the generosity to be there for others, to be close to them, so that nobody feels lonely.

After her response to God, "let it be to me according to your word" (Lk 1:38), Our Lady sets off in haste to help her cousin Elizabeth. The angel did not tell her to do this. He told her about her cousin's pregnancy as a sign of God's omnipotence. But Mary realizes that Elizabeth needs help. And she, already the Mother of God, teaches us how to show love and true friendship, by taking the initiative in self-giving and disinterested service.

The years go by, and we see Our Lady with Jesus at a wedding in Cana. There too she sees, before anyone else, what the young couple need, and again takes the initiative. The love of friendship enlightens the perspective, to see things that other people may not notice.

Later we contemplate Mary standing, steadfast, beside her Son's cross. And we ask her to help us imitate her in her capacity for being strong when we encounter other people's suffering, in order to be able to offer them the help, the balm, of sincere friendship.

After Jesus' Resurrection Our Lady gathers the apostles who had scattered following Our Lord's "Passion"; she keeps them company and consoles them.

Our Lady's life teaches us that, in our lives too, human friendship arises with new, supernatural strength on the basis of friendship with God. St. Luke says of Our Lady, "Mary kept all these things" (things which referred to Jesus), "pondering them in her heart" (Lk 2:19). Mary prays: her conversation with God is contemplation and a loving dialogue. It is friendship with God, trust in God, which overflows into self-giving to others.

21. "Melting" Into God

February 12, 1985

"He must increase, but I must decrease" (Jn 3:30).

There is a particular kind of "religious" self-centeredness, which consists of always looking at God with reference to oneself.

True contemplation certainly includes some moments of referring God to self, but its most usual action ought to be (at work, in contact with other people, and in the spiritual life) to "melt" into God, and, from God, to think of, love, and serve other people.

22. Citizens of Heaven

May 2, 1992

"He who believes in the Son has eternal life" (Jn 3:36).

Nothing in this life can diminish the real happiness of God's children; not even external adversity, obstacles, sufferings, misunderstandings, or injustice. The fact of being God's children has a definite eschatological dimension: it makes us understand with new light that what is final and permanent will come after death. The here and now is real, but it has not yet reached its fullness, the fullness of the glory of the children of God.

Everything in this life, including suffering, is saying to us that "Christ awaits us. Let us live already as 'citizens of heaven' (see Phil 3:20), being at the same time fully-fledged citizens of this earth, in the midst of difficulties, injustices, misunderstandings, but also in the midst of the joy and serenity that comes from knowing that we are beloved children of God."[12]

And death? That cannot scare Christians, nor can it cloud their radiant joy, because for God's children, death is the passage to fullness.

12. St. Josemaría, *Christ Is Passing By*, 126.

23. God in My House

February 4, 2020

"If you knew the gift of God!" (Jn 4:10).

God gives himself to those who freely love him. He enters in, takes up his abode, arranges things. The Holy Spirit starts his work of transformation: mind, will, imagination, memory, senses, passions, and desires . . . The soul and the body sometimes protest, but with God's help they let themselves be worked upon. While still being aware of our own weaknesses, we have more than once experienced faith in God with special intensity, and we don't want to lose him again.

In the process of winning the freedom to love, we discover that where our drive for individualistic possession used to predominate, now our desire to give is the stronger force. Where we used to look for our own satisfaction, now we see people to love. What is lasting rises above and conquers what is fleeting.

Chastity, a gift from God and our human response to it, grants self-mastery, guides our imagination and desires, and strengthens our freedom and our appreciation of the beauty there is in other people, within ourselves, and in things. When we master ourselves we are in a position to give ourselves totally, in celibacy or in marriage, whichever is the state to which God calls us.

Then true commitments of love are born that are worth the gift of a whole life.

God is love and wants us to be love too—including our bodies and senses, which were created by him, with all their materiality.

"Blessed are the pure in heart, for they shall see God" (Mt 5:8). We don't have to wait until the next life in order to see God: he is living in our house now, we are his temple (see 1 Cor 3:16).

24. Lovable Duty

April 17, 1977

"My food is to do the will of him who sent me, and to accomplish his work" (Jn 4:34).

What is right, what is goodness, what is the good? It is what God wants. Both in general (goodness in itself), and in particular (goodness for me, what Our Lord wants for each person).

Prayer is not only good because it is prayer (talking with God), but also because it is when, where, and how God wants us to talk to him. Mortification is more pleasing to God when it is in accordance with what he wants, because "to obey is better than sacrifice" (1 Sam 15:22).

The same applies to work. This activity is good, and therefore effective, in the measure in which it is wanted, today and now, by God. Lord, what do you want me to do? That is the question constantly asked by mature Christians. Checking and reflecting on the appropriateness, opportuneness, and effectiveness of a job or activity means checking and reflecting on what God wants.

That is the Christian virtue of obedience: loving what God wants and expects of us. His will is also made known to us through the channels of our duties and situation in the Church, in our natural or spiritual family, in our work, and in our relations with other people.

Obviously, we often don't know in specific, concrete detail what God wants of us in a given situation. However, then too we can still obey him, because always and in everything we can respond to the commandment of love; we can always try to be guided by love for him and for others. Living like that, obeying out of love, is not sterile rigidity but freedom.

Could this desire, this resolution to obey, seem excessive to us? If that were the case, it would mean we thought it excessive to identify ourselves with Jesus Christ, whose food is to do his Father's will (see Jn 4:34).

25. Freedom of Spirit

January 9, 2018

"For you were called to freedom, brethren; only do not use your freedom as an opportunity for the flesh, but through love be servants of one another" (Gal 5:13).

Acting freely, without any kind of coercion, is something that belongs to human dignity and, even more so, to the dignity of daughters and sons of God.

We can act freely in everything we do, if we do it for love. That is the meaning of St. Augustine's famous aphorism, "Love, and do what you will."[13] Freedom of spirit is this capacity and habitual attitude of acting out of love, especially in the effort to follow what God is asking of us in each circumstance: without fear of making mistakes, without fear of failing, without fear of an adverse environment. We need to get involved, with supernatural outlook, prudence, and determination, in our own social and professional sphere.

Freedom of spirit is not "an opportunity for the flesh" (Gal 5:13), nor does it mean following our own whims or resisting any and every kind of rule, because the freedom of all human beings is limited in practice by our natural duties and our acquired commitments—family, professional, civic, and more. What we need to do, instead, is to "fortify our love for a freedom that is not merely arbitrary, but is rendered truly human by acknowledgment of the good that underlies it"[14]—a freedom that is reconciled with God.

Growing in love means growing in freedom of spirit, being freer. In St. Thomas Aquinas' words, "The more intense our charity is, the freer we are."[15]

---

13. St. Augustine, *Homilies on the Letter of St. Jn to the Parthians*, VII, 8.
14. Pope Benedict XVI, *Caritas in veritate*, 68.
15. St. Thomas Aquinas, *Commentary on the Sentences*, III, d.29, a.8, qla.3.

June 26, 2019

"The people pressed upon him to hear the word of God, as he was standing by the lake of Gennesaret" (Lk 5:1).

People cluster around Jesus because they are constantly searching for good, beautiful things that will fill their hearts. We all have, in the depths of our souls, longings that only he is capable of satisfying.

We hear so often of people who, on discovering the happiness that properly belongs to a Christian life, exclaim, "But I never realized! Nobody told me that! I thought it was something different!"

Lord, make us capable of recognizing that longing for your face, those signs of thirst for you, in other people. May we learn how to pass on your true image to the people around us.

May we pass on the image of Christ who puts out a little from the shore so that everyone, even those furthest away, can see and hear him.

27. Going Out to Meet Our Contemporaries
July 7, 2017

"[Jesus] said to Simon, 'Put out into the deep'" (Lk 5:4).

Faced with the challenges of this world of ours, which are both complex and exciting, what is Our Lord expecting of us Christians today? He wants us to go out to meet people's anxieties and needs, in order to bring the Gospel, in its original purity and its radiant newness, to everyone.

The dimensions of this task are outlined by two fishing scenes from the Sea of Tiberias which offer a glimpse of the way Christians navigate through history. One is the Master's forceful invitation to be daring—"Put out into the deep!" (Lk 5:4) and the other is the Beloved Apostle's exclamation "It is the Lord!" (Jn 21:7), reflecting the attentive, perceptive faithfulness that enables us to recognize Jesus.

Putting out into the deep sea of this world does not mean adapting the message or the spirit to current events, because the Gospel has the capacity to shed its own light on all situations.

Instead, it summons each of us, with our spiritual and intellectual resources, with our professional skills or life experiences, and also with our limitations and defects, to try and see how we can cooperate more and more in the huge task of setting Christ at the summit of all human activities.

To do this we need in-depth knowledge of the time we live in, its dynamics and potential, and also of the limitations and injustices, sometimes serious ones, that afflict it. Above all, we need personal union with Jesus in prayer and the sacraments. This way we will be able to remain open to the action of the Holy Spirit, in order to call, with charity, at the door of our contemporaries' hearts.

June 26, 2017

"Let down your nets for a catch" (Lk 5:4).

Jesus comes out to meet us as he went out in search of his first disciples by the Sea of Galilee. He enters into our lives just as he got into Peter's boat.

And the same boat that had witnessed a professional failure—a fishing trip when they hadn't caught anything—now becomes the Teacher's professorial chair, the place from which he reveals the mysteries of God's kingdom. And even more: in that same boat there begins a supernatural adventure, prefigured by the miraculous catch of fish.

Christ's presence transforms our old boat, our work, into the place of God's action. Our Lord asks us to be instruments in his hands to bring joy and happiness to this world which needs him so badly. And that can be done with little deeds that are very simple, but full of charity.

He invites us, as he invited Peter: "Put out into the deep, and let down your nets for a catch" (Lk 5:4). The nets this time are let down into our work, now impregnated with God's grace, and so transformed into a place of Christian witness, of sincere help for our coworkers and everyone we come in contact with.

Along the same lines, we can recall Pope Francis' invitation: "When your efforts to reawaken faith in your friends seem to be in vain, like the nocturnal efforts of the fishermen, remember that with Jesus everything changes. The word of the Lord filled the nets, and the word of the Lord makes the missionary work of his disciples effective."[16]

---

16. Pope Francis, Address to young people, September 22, 2013.

29. Young at Heart: Facing Forward

October 6, 2017

"We toiled all night and took nothing! But at your word I will let down the nets" (Lk 5:5).

We can say to Jesus in prayer, "I've been fighting to improve for years, and you can just see, Lord, what I'm like. But now, trusting in your word, I'm going to launch out into the deep, toward the holiness that is not the absence of defects but perfection in love, in being identified with you. At your word," we can say with St. Peter, "I will let down the nets."

St. Josemaría often said that in 1928 all he had was 26 years of age, God's grace, and cheerfulness. It was his youthful spirit that kept alive his desire to learn and to grow, and ours should lead us to want to begin again and again. So we should never let discouragement enter our souls, but nurture a desire to keep facing forward. Grant us, Lord, this youthful spirit.

God's grace! A share in the divine life of the Blessed Trinity, as sons and daughters of God the Father in Christ through the Holy Spirit. Our Lord offers this life to us constantly, above all in the Eucharist, in the sacrament of penance, and in prayer. How much we learn from that offering! How often St. Josemaría exhorted us with word and example to be Eucharistic souls, souls of prayer!

Cheerfulness! It leads us to see the positive side, even the funny side, of things. We also need to have a sense of humor when confronted with our own limitations—this is a consequence of the joy of being God's children. We will be happy, no matter what happens, to the extent of our faith in the love God has for us.

September 18, 2018

"Jesus said to Simon, 'Do not be afraid; henceforth you will be catching men'" (Lk 5:10).

With these words Christ changes Simon's whole life. From now on the Galilean fisherman knows what he is alive for. Like him, every single person sooner or later faces the question "What is my mission in life?" We all have a divine vocation, we are all called by God to union with him.

Faith is a powerful light that can illuminate our future and inspire desires for fulfilment. At a time in life when maybe our childhood certainties are being shaken, and the light of faith may also be weakened, we need to recall the deepest truth about ourselves: that we are God's children, and that we were created out of love.

God makes the most radical call: he calls each and every one of us to be fully happy with him. The Creator does not just toss us into life and forget about us; the One who creates also loves and calls. Therefore the discernment of our particular path needs to be illuminated by faith in God's love for us.

"Do not be afraid," Jesus says to Peter. Our personal search may give rise to a sort of inner turbulence, as the prospect of freedom makes us feel dizzy. Will I be happy? Will I have the strength to do it? Is it worthwhile committing myself? Here too, God does not leave us alone. He will inspire us if we learn to listen to him. We ask him for this every time we pray, "Thy will be done on earth as it is in heaven—may your will be done in me, in everyone, in each of us.

31. Their Home, Their Task, Their Native Land

June 26, 2019

"And when they had brought their boats to land, they left everything and followed him" (Lk 5:11).

Jesus invited Peter, James, and John to follow him as his disciples. Their answer was a decided "yes."

It is impressive to reflect how, just a few years later, their apostolic zeal had taken the Good News to many of the most important places in the world of their time, including Rome.

The early Christians, in spite of facing persecutions and misunderstandings, knew that the world belonged to them, that it was their home, their task, their native land.

Knowing that we are God's children, summoned by him, we can never feel like foreigners in our own house; we cannot go through this life like visitors in a strange place, nor can we go along our streets fearfully, like someone on unknown ground.

The world is ours because it belongs to our Father God.

We are called to love this world, not a different one where we think maybe we'd fit in better. We have to love the real people around us, in the specific challenges that we face.

32. Joy

February 29, 2020

"Rejoice and be glad, for your reward is great in heaven" (Mt 5:12).

In the Beatitudes (Mt 5:1–12; Lk 6:20–26), Jesus Christ gives us the keys that open the gates of heaven . . . and the gateway to happiness on this earth.

"The poor in spirit" know that they are needy. They don't trust in their own virtues or possessions, but abandon themselves in God's gifts. Following the path of humility, they experience the joy of God's fatherly embrace.

The tears of "those who mourn" are primarily sorrow for offenses against God: lack of love, infidelities, injustices. People who mourn in this way achieve the happiness of God's consolation.

"The meek" are happy on earth: no adversity, no human setback, brings them down. Imitating Christ, they retain their peace of mind and serenity.

"Those who hunger and thirst for righteousness" try to put God's will into practice. And by doing so they achieve a fullness that does not satiate or cloy, because it comes from God.

"The merciful" see other people's sorrows and defects through Christ's eyes; they make room for them in their hearts. They also understand and forgive. By their mercifulness, they obtain the joy of mercy for themselves.

"The pure in heart" discover unsuspected panoramas of intimacy with God and quality in their relationships with other people. And they rejoice in that sight.

"The peacemakers" receive the blessing of peace—Christ's peace (see Eph 2:14)—for themselves, and sow around them the joy of God's children. They try to avoid pointless arguing, to overcome irritation and hastiness, to be positive, and to spread optimism and hope.

"Those who are persecuted" for the love of God, and who fulfill his will, have their reward in heaven, which is also joy on earth.

"The Beatitudes always bring you to joy. They are the paths to reach joy."[17]

17. Pope Francis, General Audience, January 29, 2020.

33. The Actions of God's Children

April 20, 1992

"Pray then like this: 'Our Father who art in heaven'" (Mt 6:9).

By supernatural grace we are God's children in Jesus Christ; we become "conformed to the image of his Son, in order that he might be the first-born among many brethren" (Rom 8:29).

The fact of having God for our Father is a radical characteristic of our dialogue with God—our prayer—and the way we practice all the Christian virtues. By God's mercy, it also characterizes us as citizens of heaven.

Let's say it again: our faith is the faith of God's children; our prayer is the prayer of God's children; our joy is the joy of God's children; our fortitude is the fortitude of God's children . . .

God's will for each of us is summarized in this: "What the Lord asks of you is that you should, at every moment, act as children and servants of his."[18]

---

18. St. Josemaría, *Christ Is Passing By*, 60.

34. The Secret of Youth
October 1, 2018

"For where your treasure is, there will your heart be also" (Mt 6:21).

A heart that is young and in love is capable of renewing itself and living out the Christian vocation and apostolic mission joyfully, even amidst setbacks and suffering.

St. Josemaría explained the secret of his vitality as follows: "When I pray at the foot of the altar 'to God who gives joy to my youth' (see Ps 42:4), I feel young and I know that I will never consider myself old. If I keep true to my God, Love will constantly vivify me. My youth will be renewed like that of the eagle (see Ps 102:5)."[19] If we are constantly united to Our Lord we will always be young, and we will work together with him to build up the Church, ever old and ever new, in many different places, cultures and times.

---

19. St. Josemaría, *Friends of God*, 31.

November 1, 2019

"The good man out of the good treasure of his heart produces good, and the evil man out of his evil treasure produces evil; for out of the abundance of the heart his mouth speaks" (Lk 6:45).

St. Josemaría taught us the specific way by which God invites us to announce the Gospel in the middle of the world. "You have to bring souls close to God with the appropriate words, which will awaken apostolic horizons; with discreet advice, which helps them to look at a problem in a Christian way; with a friendly conversation, which shows them how to practice charity; through an apostolate which I have sometimes called the apostolate of friendship and trust."[20]

True friendship—like charity, which raises the human dimension of friendship to the supernatural plane—is a value in itself. It is not a means or an instrument for gaining any social advantage, even though it may bring such advantages (as it may also bring disadvantages). Friendship has an intrinsic value because it denotes a sincere concern for the other person. It is a dialogue in which we give and receive light. In friendship plans are forged as we mutually open up new horizons. In friendship we rejoice in what is good and support one another in what is difficult; we have a good time together, since God wants us to be happy.

When friendship is like that, loyal and sincere, there is no way it can be instrumentalized. Each friend simply wants to pass on to the other the good they experience in their own life. Normally we will do this without even realizing it, through our

20. St. Josemaría, Letter dated 24 March 1930, 11.

example, our joy, and a desire to serve that is expressed in a thousand little ways. Nevertheless, "[t]he importance of witness does not mean that we should be silent about the word. Why should we not speak of Jesus, why should we not tell others that he gives us strength in life, that we enjoy talking with him, that we benefit from meditating on his words?"[21]

And then, naturally, friendship ends up in personal confidences, full of sensitive respect for freedom, as a necessary result of the genuineness of that friendship.

21. Pope Francis, *Christus Vivit*, Rome, 25 March 2019, 176.

February 4, 2020

"And when the Lord saw her, he had compassion on her and said to her, 'Do not weep'" (Lk 7:13).

Friendship means happiness, but also suffering: sickness, deaths, disappointments, life crises, family conflicts . . . As Pope St. Paul VI said, "The art of loving often transforms itself into the art of suffering."[22] It is the other side of the coin of friendship, and being there for people at such times is a proof that friendship is genuine.

Compassion increases at the same pace as our love for God, which clothes us in his feelings and clarifies our vision. It is astonishing to see how deeply Christ is moved on meeting the funeral procession of the son of the widow at Nain. "When the Lord saw her, he had compassion on her and said to her, 'Do not weep'" (Lk 7:13).

Like love, compassion is creative and expresses a desire to make our friend's suffering our own, in order to lighten it, with words, silences, listening, actions, presence, remembering, prayer, acts of service . . . At the same time it extends to everyone. From the Cross, Jesus had compassion on, and offered himself in sacrifice for, the whole human race, transcending time and space.

We get to a point where we would want to comfort the sufferings of every single person in the whole world. We experience the paradox, within ourselves, of freely-given Love that has opened our eyes to other people's needs and our own inability to provide a solution to everything. Then we understand that only Jesus is "the way, and the truth, and the life" (Jn 14:6), not us.

---

22. St. Paul VI, Speech at the opening of the fourth session of the Council, Rome, AAS 57, 1965, 794–805.

37. Openness
November 1, 2019

"When the Pharisees saw this, they said to his disciples, 'Why does your teacher eat with tax collectors and sinners?'" (Mt 9:11).

The Pharisees criticize Jesus, as though being a friend of tax collectors and sinners (Mt 11:19) were something bad. Christ's friendship doesn't exclude anyone.

Striving to imitate Our Lord, within our own littleness, we too shouldn't exclude anyone, but should love everyone in Jesus Christ, with sincere friendship, no matter what their personal situation is.

Let's contemplate Jesus' example. Our Lord doesn't limit his contacts to a small group. He spends time with everyone, "with the holy women, and with large crowds; with representatives of Israel's highest social strata, like Nicodemus, and with the publican Zacchaeus; with people reputed pious, and with sinners like the Samaritan woman; with the sick and the healthy; with the poor, whom he loved with his whole heart; with doctors of the law, and with Gentiles whose faith he praises above Israel's; with the elderly and with children. Jesus is ready to speak to everyone. And his words heal, console, and enlighten. How often I have meditated personally, and have had others meditate, on Christ's apostolic manner, which is so human and so divine, built as it is upon friendship and confidence!"[23]

23. St. Josemaría, Letter dated 24 October 1965, 10.

38. Understanding

November 1, 2019

"A friend of tax collectors and sinners" (Mt 11:19).

Friendship is especially valuable for that necessary sign of charity which is understanding others. "True friendship also means making a heartfelt effort to understand the convictions of our friends, even though we may never come to share them or accept them."[24]

Thus our friends help us to understand ways of viewing life that are different from our own, that enrich our inner world, and, when the friendship is deep, that enable us to experience the world in a different way. This is, in the end, a true sharing in others' sentiments, which is sharing in their life and in their experiences.

To build true friendship, we need to develop the capacity to look at other people with affection, to the point where we see them through Christ's eyes.

---

24. St. Josemaría, *Furrow*, 746.

39. Discrepancy
February 25, 1997

"And he said to her, 'Your sins are forgiven.'" (Lk 7:48).

What a huge discrepancy there is between our sins, however numerous and serious, and the simplicity of a brief confession—a few words—and absolution, through which those sins cease to exist.

But that discrepancy is only apparent, because behind something so simple (the few essential words of confession and absolution) there stands, making it effective, nothing less than the Incarnation, life, Passion, Death, and Resurrection of Our Lord Jesus Christ.

How great you are, Lord, and how immense your wisdom and mercy toward us are!

40. Good Soil

January 5, 2020

"Other seeds fell on good soil and brought forth grain, some a hundredfold, some sixty, some thirty" (Mt 13:8).

At the beginning of a new year St. Josemaría used to say, "New year, new struggle!" This struggle demands an effort, it's true, but above all it needs God's grace. Let's look at the parable of the sower, and desire to be "good soil" to receive God's gift, the seed that will bear abundant fruit. Jesus offers us that gift every day in the Holy Eucharist.

In the synagogue at Capernaum, Our Lord says, "Unless you eat the flesh of the Son of man and drink his blood, you have no life in you" (Jn 6:53). Let's liven up, with greater depth and gratitude, our faith in God's love for us (see 1 Jn 4:16)—a love that becomes sacramentally visible to us in the Holy Eucharist. This way we can properly guide our struggle to be "good soil" that welcomes the seed.

Let's keep our eyes on Jesus Christ, who, although we are so worthless, wants to fill us with renewed effectiveness and joy.

41. Putting God First
October 1, 2018

"And he said, 'The kingdom of God is as if a man should scatter seed upon the ground, and should sleep and rise night and day, and the seed should sprout and grow, he knows not how. The earth produces of itself, first the blade, then the ear, then the full grain in the ear'" (Mk 4:26–28).

The words of the Gospel lead us to consider the primacy of God's role in all evangelization. St. Josemaría made it clear to us when talking about Opus Dei. He played his part in taking it forward, in the conviction that all the drive that moved him to serve souls came from God. "Lord, I thank you for having made me understand without a shadow of doubt that everything is yours: the blossoms, the fruit, the tree, the leaves, and the clear water which springs up to eternal life. *Gratias tibi, Deus!*—thank you, God!"[25] The primacy of God's grace is equally real in the life of each and every one of us.

Besides reflecting on God's gift let us renew our thanksgiving because, despite our own littleness, he has wanted to rely on us in order to make us his coworkers (see 2 Cor 6:1).

At times it might seem that, in reality, our role in carrying out God's plans is irrelevant. Nevertheless, he takes our freedom seriously and truly relies on us. Let us recall that young boy who placed the little that he had—five loaves of bread and two fish—in Jesus' hands. Thanks to this small act of generosity, Christ fed a multitude (see Jn 6:1–13).

God also counts on our daily response, made up of small things that become great through the strength of his grace.

---

25. St. Josemaría, *In Dialogue with the Lord*, 125.

42. Abandonment in God

April 20, 1991

"But even the hairs of your head are all numbered" (Mt 10:30).

Abandonment in God is not possible unless God himself grants it to us. He wants to grant it, but meets the obstacle of our ego.

When faced with a disconcerting situation, let us make acts of abandonment, such as this prayer of St. Josemaría's: "My Lord and my God: into your hands I abandon the past, the present, and the future: small and great, little and big, temporal and eternal."

Let's not be surprised if we suffer interiorly when God tears out our false self-security from our soul by its roots. Let's say, "Thank you, Lord!"

Let's make an effort to think about others, decentering our attention from ourselves and our own concerns.

Lord, I want to see your face (see Ps 27:8).

43. Seeing

December 12, 1994

"As he landed he saw a great throng, and he had compassion on them" (Mk 6:34).

Christ's gaze is penetrating, deep, and compassionate. St. Josemaría would supplicate Our Lord with the emotional plea, "May I see with your eyes, my own Christ, my dearest Jesus!"

"Lord," we can pray, "I need to see with your eyes; to see the world, each person, each situation, my own life . . ., as you see them.

"May I see with your eyes, Jesus, to perceive what there is in me that needs to be uprooted, added, or improved, in the light of the fact that I have God for my Father.

"May I see with your eyes, to discover how to help the people you have placed near me so that we can each look out for one another; how to support every one of my brothers and sisters.

"May I see, through your eyes, how to improve my work and each particular thing I have to tackle."

Let's learn to repeat, with new meaning, the cry of the blind man, Bartimaeus: "Master, let me receive my sight!" *Domine, ut videam!* (Mk 10:51). And then extend it to others: "Lord, may we see! May they see!" *Domine, ut videamus! Ut videant!*

44. Joy without Fear

January 26, 1988

"Take heart, it is I; have no fear" (Mt 14:27).

"Only love that is almighty can ground a joy that is free from anxiety."[26]

When joy is too "human," it always includes some element of fear, if only fear that the joy will cease.

It can, and sometimes does, happen that even the supernatural joy of meeting Christ includes fear: a sort of fear of our own littleness, fear of forgetting the basis of that joy, which is nothing other than the love that God has for us.

Resolution: "supernaturalize" all our joys, and especially the habit of joy that expels all fear. And then we will recover the joy of God's children, which is total trust in him with no sense of fear at all.

26. Joseph Ratzinger, "The Ground of our Freedom", in *Seek That Which Is Above*, Ignatius Press, 2007, p.44.

45. Nourishment

March 11, 2004

"Do not labor for the food which perishes, but for the food which endures to eternal life" (Jn 6:27).

Jesus is hidden in the Blessed Eucharist. "O Godhead hid, devoutly I adore you, who truly are within the forms before me," sings the hymn *Adoro Te Devote.*

But in reality the Eucharist—the "clothing" in which Christ presents himself to us, the sacramental species—shows him to us as what he wants to be for every single person: food, nourishment.

It is a food into which history is "condensed." An ancient prayer that the Church uses for Vespers on the Solemnity of Corpus Christi says of the Eucharist *recolitur memoria Passionis eius,* "it recalls the memory of Christ's Passion" (the past), *mens impletur gratia,* "the soul is filled with grace" (the present), *et futurae gloriae nobis pignus datur,* "and the pledge of future glory is given to us" (the eschatological future).

Let us go to the Eucharist with the desire to identify ourselves with Jesus (Christ himself) and to "condense" into it all the moments of each day. Then we too will become nourishment, help and support for others.

March 19, 2018

"Is not this Jesus, the son of Joseph, whose father and mother we know?" (Jn 6:42).

In the simplicity and greatness of St. Joseph—a craftsman, like so many others—we discern the features of those who understand that they are called by God to live close to him in their daily lives, with everything this involves, including unforeseen events and worries.

St. Joseph lived under the same roof as God. We could think that in this respect he doesn't seem to be "like other craftsmen" after all. But don't we ourselves pray: "Lord, I am not worthy that you should enter under my roof"? And if we let him, he enters. A single word of his is enough to heal us (see Mt 8:8).

Today especially, with the whole Church, we contemplate St. Joseph, that just and faithful man. Let us entrust ourselves to his intercession, so that he might help us respond to Christ's immense love every day, opening wide the doors of our house, of our heart, to him. And we ask that this response may spur us to ever greater service to those around us, spreading the joy of the Gospel.

47. Doing Our Own Work

May 13, 1989

"All are yours; and you are Christ's; and Christ is God's" (1 Cor 3:22–23).

If we look at our lives with the eyes of faith, we'll realize that nothing in it falls outside of God's will. Our work is also a major area for sanctification, a place where we can seek Christ and find Christ. The founder of Opus Dei talked about sanctifying our work, sanctifying ourselves in our work, and sanctifying others through our work.[27]

If we try to identify ourselves with Christ while we are engaged in any kind of activity, no matter what it is we'll be doing *our own* work; that activity will be work that belongs to God, and we are God's children.

Working well doesn't only mean trying to do things well, but also ensuring that all the dimensions of that work are good: the thing that is done, our relations with other people as we work (smiling when we are tired, standing in for a coworker who needs it, helping someone who is struggling with a back-log . . .), and our relationship with God in that work.

At the human level, working well means not being content with doing what has to be done, but being proactive, tackling first something that matters to other people, following up important questions, and so on.

At the supernatural level, how much it can help us to unite our work explicitly to the Blessed Eucharist! In the mystery of the altar, the wheat and the grapes symbolize the world, this earth; we also offer our work, to unite it to Christ's sacrifice.

---

27. See St. Josemaría, *Christ Is Passing By*, 45.

And then, through that work, we're cooperating in "sanc-tifying others with our work."

48. Cooperators with Christ

March 9, 2006

"Be steadfast, immovable, always abounding in the work of the Lord, knowing that in the Lord your labor is not in vain" (1 Cor 15:58).

All honest human realities, all jobs, can and should be a path to and a means of holiness, a meeting with Jesus Christ. "Work is born of love, manifests love, and is ordained to love."[28] Sanctifying work, any honest work, means doing it for God and for other people, no matter what the work itself may consist of.

When undertaking our work—any task that "lands on top of us," whether pleasant or hard, clearly effective, or seemingly pointless—let's realize that all work is born of God's love for us.

Let's thank Our Lord for the fact that in this activity, here and now, he wants us to be cooperators with him, at least because through it, we can show a little of his love to other people. We'll become convinced that in the Lord, no work is in vain.

---

28. St. Josemaría, *Christ Is Passing By*, 48.

49. Center and Root

May 7, 1985

"He who eats my flesh and drinks my blood abides in me, and I in him" (Jn 6:56).

Our desire to remain in Christ is shown especially by love for the Mass, which is "the center and the root of a Christian's spiritual life."[29]

The Mass is the root; it is necessarily. In the Sacrifice of the Eucharist, the work of our redemption is made present; in it is the source of grace, peace, mercy, and effectiveness. A spiritual way rooted in the Eucharist contains all that is most valuable in effecting our developing identification with Jesus Christ.

The Mass is the center: it should be the center not only objectively but also subjectively, with a habitual, often-renewed awareness that what is most important at every moment is the fact that I have celebrated or am going to celebrate Mass; that I have been at or am going to be at Mass.

This constant reference to the Mass is a gift from God, rather than the result of human effort; a gift which will reach us through Our Blessed Lady's motherly mediation.

---

29. St. Josemaría, *Christ Is Passing By*, 87.

50. Malicious Gossip Normalized

March 20, 2015

"What comes out of the mouth proceeds from the heart" (Mt 15:18).

Other people's good name, their good reputation, is a precious possession protected by charity and justice.

The "normalization" and spread of malicious gossip, in the private and the public spheres, creates a climate of suspicion and uncertainty in personal, family, and social relations, which damages them greatly.

Sometimes people are aware that they are causing harm, and many other times they are driven by vanity, the excuse of "meaning well," and in general, the urge to talk unrestrainedly that comes of accepting, interiorizing, the normalization of slander.

Our tongues also need to be transformed and purified. Our tongues give sound to the music playing in our hearts.

Rather than stopping to think about how we talk, we could ask ourselves, "What is there in my heart? Do I judge people interiorly? What do I want and expect from my peers? What do they expect from me? Do I try to look at other people as I'd like them to look at me? Do I see them as created by God, and as children of God?"

51. With Your Help

January 30, 1986

"She came and knelt before him, saying, 'Lord, help me!'" (Mt 15:25).

When we meet some small opportunity for self-giving, mortification, or service, and we think, "I don't care," we need to realize that Our Lord does care, and that it matters for us and for other people.

At the same time, we have learned from experience over time, that our good desires, good resolutions, and great ideas, are often demolished by our own weakness. That weakness is a weakness of the will, and it stops us from wanting seriously enough.

So on the one hand, let's ask Our Lord for the grace never to think "I don't care" about the things he asks us for, or about other people's needs.

And at the same time, when we receive a clear light, when we make a firm resolution to say "yes," let's always add, "Lord, with your grace! My Mother, with your help!"

Then those resolutions, repeated over and over again, will be new, because we are convinced we need heaven's help; not repetition, but renewal. New again: *nunc coepi!*—now I begin! Lord, may renewal be love.

52. Jesus' Promise

September 1, 2018

"And I tell you, you are Peter, and on this rock I will build my church, and the powers of death shall not prevail against it" (Mt 16:18).

This is Jesus' promise, which we hear every year in the Gospel of the Mass on the Solemnity of St. Peter and St. Paul. These words remind me of the spiritual path that St. Josemaría suggested from very early on: *Omnes cum Petro ad Iesum per Mariam*—all together with Peter to Jesus through Mary.

Let's love the Church and the Pope more and more. We will find it helpful to remember that the Church is not simply an assembly of men and women that we have joined. Rather, and above all, the Church is "Christ present in our midst, God coming toward mankind to save us, calling us with his revelation, sanctifying us with his grace, sustaining us with his constant help, in the great and small battles of our daily life."[30]

From the time of the apostles onwards, the Church has suffered, and is still suffering, persecutions and also attacks on her unity from within. This fact, far from discouraging us, should lead us to an ever-renewed outlook of faith, which is a gift from God, shown in prayer for the Church, the Pope, and especially for all who suffer persecution for the sake of the Gospel.

---

30. St. Josemaría, *Christ Is Passing By*, 131.

53. The Present Transfigured

August 6, 1987

"And as he was praying, the appearance of his countenance was altered, and his raiment became dazzling white" (Lk 9:29).

In the Transfiguration Jesus revealed to Peter, James, and John a foretaste of future glory. Peter wished to remain in the future glory permanently—"Master, it is well that we are here; let us make three booths . . ." (Lk 9:33).

We naturally want to be completely happy, but complete happiness is only achievable in glory, with the vision of God. We can understand why the psalmist—and we with him—addressed the Lord with a wish that is at the same time a resolution: "Thy face, Lord, do I seek" (Ps 27:8). We also seek God's face now, through prayer, but we don't try to escape from a present that, like the past and the future, we can't always control.

Prayer: contemplating God, talking, and listening to him. Far from taking us out of the world, it situates us firmly in the reality of here and now, and moves us to love in a way that changes and converts us. The present itself is transfigured.

With the cooperation of human freedom, God's grace transfigures us, transforming us into children of God, into Christ's likeness, as St. Paul writes: "We . . . are being changed into his likeness from one degree of glory to another; for this comes from the Lord who is the Spirit" (2 Cor 3:18).

During the Transfiguration Jesus was speaking with Moses and Elijah about his forthcoming Passion in Jerusalem. Glory and cross. We learn to love the cross of every day and we recover the radiance of peace and joy. Then we can sum up Christian life, and every moment in it, in St. Josemaría's words: "from the Cross, with Christ, to the immortal glory of the Father."[31]

---

31. St. Josemaría, "Instruction," 19 March 1934, 29.

54. Without Him We Can Do Nothing

March 8, 1979

"The apostles said to the Lord, 'Increase our faith!'" (Lk 17:5).

We too beg Jesus, "Increase our faith, hope and charity."

It isn't enough to know in theory that everything that happens to us is for our good, that God is our Father—my Father—that Our Lord and Mary are there for us, and that "I can do all things in him who strengthens me" (Phil 4:13).

It isn't enough to know in theory that whatever happens, and despite our obvious and undeniable failings, we shall be victorious with Christ.

It isn't enough to know in theory that it's only worthwhile loving God, and in him, everyone else.

We need that knowledge to be supernatural; we need you, Lord, to give it to us, specifically and permanently, because we are convinced of what you told us: "apart from me you can do nothing" (Jn 15:5).

Without you, Lord, we can't truly believe. We want to believe your word, everything that you have revealed to us and that the Church's magisterium tells us. And in consequence, to live in justice: "He who through faith is righteous shall live" (Rom 1:17).

Without you, Lord, we can't truly hope. We want to place our trust in your promises, helped by the Holy Spirit's grace and power. And to live on earth with the perspective of the happiness we will find finally and permanently in heaven.

Without you, Lord, we can't truly love either. We want to put everything that concerns you in first place, and to love each and every person for love of you. To go through life trying to love one another as you have loved us (see Jn 15:12).

55. Faith in Mercy
April 8, 2018

"And the Lord said, 'If you had faith as a grain of mustard seed, you could say to this sycamine tree, "Be rooted up, and be planted in the sea," and it would obey you'" (Lk 17:6).

On Divine Mercy Sunday, with the joy of the Easter season, the liturgy reminds us of St. John's words: "This is the victory that overcomes the world, our faith" (1 Jn 5:4).

In the thrilling mission of bringing the Gospel to every nation, every environment, and every person, all of us in the Church encounter many joys, but also many difficulties.

We will remain happy and filled with hope if we live by faith in Divine Mercy. We cannot attain this faith by our own efforts, but, especially when we feel weak, we can ask Jesus for it like the apostles did: "Increase our faith!" (Lk 17:5).

56. Lukewarmness

March 12, 2003

"So, because you are lukewarm, and neither cold nor hot, I will spew you out of my mouth" (Rev 3:16).

Lukewarmness is a lack of love, a cooling off of charity, which gets muddied by neglect and laziness.

The lack of love results from a lack of faith, because faith works through charity; faith that it really is worthwhile giving ourselves totally, without holding anything back.

Lukewarmness is also a lack of hope—hope in our wonderful destination, which is glory.

February 14, 2017

"Teacher, we saw a man casting out demons in your name, and we forbade him, because he was not following us" (Mk 9:38).

Loving the world in order to transform it means going arm in arm with everyone. It means we each need to acquire deep human, professional, and doctrinal formation, according to our possibilities, and it demands a strong presence in the forums where ideas are discussed, with an open mentality that will enable us to dialogue with everyone.

We also need a certain degree of influence, which we acquire if we take others seriously, and a personal "gift of tongues." This will foster the sort of empathy which makes the Christian view of reality convincing, because it makes us aware of the existential questions of our neighbor, and keeps us from becoming strident or falling into a monologue.

Respect for the dignity of every person despite their errors, and for the common good of society, plus calm, responsible work in collaboration with other citizens, make manifest the beauty and attractiveness of Christian values.

Part of our mission in the great family of God's sons and daughters that is the Church, is to increase mutual appreciation among the faithful in the Church and all the very varied groups that can exist there. "The principal apostolate we Christians must carry out in the world, and the best witness we can give of our faith, is to help bring about a climate of genuine charity within the Church."[32]

32. St. Josemaría, *Friends of God*, 226.

58. Living Stones

March 26, 1979

"For where two or three are gathered in my name, there am I in the midst of them" (Mt 18:20).

When Our Lord calls us to carry out a specific evangelizing task, an apostolic work, the key is not to build things, nor to write things—plans, programs, or goals. It is to help build up souls, "living stones."

The mission to spread the Church is, first of all and always, an apostolate with souls, loving everyone sincerely; trying to ensure that our example, words, prayer, and sacrifice help other souls—specific people, with names and surnames—to achieve the happiness of God by meeting Jesus Christ.

Only in that light does everything else acquire value and meaning; promoting apostolic projects, plans for evangelizing, and so on. And personal apostolate, and fraternal correction, are seen in their true dimensions. If we were to forget that, all our apostolic buildings, projects, and works would have no soul.

This is what following Christ's example and mission means; developing the Church that he founded, first and fundamentally in souls: in Peter, John, James . . . and all the others.

January 9, 2018

"The truth will make you free" (Jn 8:32).

All the promises of liberation that have followed one upon another throughout the centuries are true to the extent that they are nourished by the truth about God and man. And this Truth is a person: Jesus, the Way, the Truth, and the Life (see Jn 14:6).

St. John Paul II reminds us that "today also, even after two thousand years, we see Christ as the one who brings man freedom based on truth, frees man from what curtails, diminishes, and as it were breaks off this freedom at its root, in man's soul, his heart and his conscience."[33]

To discover the deepest meaning of freedom we have to contemplate Jesus Christ, who "gives himself up to death with the full freedom of Love."[34] His freedom unfolds continuously throughout his life on earth, right up to the sacrifice of the Cross. "I lay down my life, that I may take it again. No one takes it from me, but I lay it down of my own accord" (Jn 10:17–18).

"The Lord lived the crowning point of his freedom on the Cross as a summit of love. When they shouted at him on Calvary: 'If you are the Son of God, come down from the Cross!' he showed his freedom as the Son precisely by remaining on that scaffold, to do the Father's merciful will to the very end."[35]

By sacrificing himself freely, for love, Jesus Christ has obtained for us the freedom of God's children forever. It is not a temporary gift, to employ only during our life here on earth. Freedom, like love, "never ends" (1 Cor 13:8). In heaven our

33. St. John Paul II, *Redemptor Hominis*, Rome, March 4, 1979, 12.
34. St. Josemaría, *The Way of the Cross*, Tenth Station.
35. Pope Benedict XVI, Angelus address, Rome, July 1, 2007.

freedom not only won't disappear, but rather will attain its fullness in embracing God's Love.

Our path there is a path toward "the glorious liberty of the children of God" (Rom 8:21).

60. What Do They Need?

March 13, 2003

"He set him on his own beast and brought him to an inn, and took care of him" (Lk 10:34).

We can be selfish even in serving others, particularly when we see someone in need and our approach is "What do I have to do? What is my duty here?"

God grant that in that situation our first reaction might be to think what the other person needs, what will be best for them, what will make them happy.

For instance, if there's a traffic accident and people are hurt, may we think, "What do they need?" Like the Good Samaritan, who didn't think about what he was obliged to do but what the injured man needed, and anointed his wounds with oil and wine, took him to an inn, and paid the innkeeper in advance.

Loving others radically means seeing them as a gift God makes me; but not for my service or my benefit, but for their sake—loving them as God does, for themselves.

61. Souls of Prayer

October 15, 1996

"'Lord, teach us to pray, as John taught his disciples.' And he said to them, 'When you pray, say: "Father, hallowed be thy name . . ."'" (Lk 11:1).

Our divine filiation—having God for our Father—leads us to prayer; among other reasons (and in fact fundamentally) because being God's children means that we are identified with Christ, the Son, the Word of the eternal, intra-Trinitarian dialogue.

Lord, may we not get used to difficulties in prayer. Help us to say *nunc coepi!*—now I begin—as we fight, really asking you for help, relying on Our Lady, St. Joseph, our Guardian Angel . . .

And that conversation with Our Lord will produce the strength to turn all our actions, especially our work, into prayer.

Filial prayer is trusting: "My Lord and my God: into your hands I abandon everything, past, present, and future: small and great, little and big, temporal and eternal."

Being souls of prayer, and divine filiation, go together; because Christian prayer should always be the prayer of God's children.

62. Wretchedness and Greatness

July 16, 1984

"And [the prodigal son] arose and came to his father" (Lk 15:20).

Humility "helps us to recognize, at one and the same time, both our wretchedness and our greatness."[36] Both are clearly apparent in the Prodigal Son.

In a way, it would be egocentric to look only at our failings; it would mean not knowing, or ignoring, the deepest truth of our being, our human condition.

So when our own weakness, mistakes, and limitations become especially obvious, humility demands that, at the same time, we consider our greatness: at our divine filiation, the abiding fact that we are children of God.

That leaves no room for pessimism or sadness.

Then awareness of our own nothingness is joined to daring, magnanimity, optimism, and security in the victory that comes from our Father God. He is always waiting for us, like the father in the parable, to come out to meet us and cover us with signs of affection.

36. St. Josemaría, *Friends of God*, 94.

63. Conversion
June 20, 1992

"But while he was yet at a distance, his father saw him and had compassion, and ran and embraced him and kissed him" (Lk 15:20).

Our weakness is the usual setting of our journey toward the Father, of our trajectory toward the fullness of glory of God's children.

This can only be understood in the light of God's mercy. This setting for our lives, the setting of personal weakness and sin, is in fact the setting for the mercy of our Father God, who stirs us up and draws us continually toward himself. It's the setting for us to go to and return to the Father; the setting for our conversion.

Conversion, repentance, are not things that only come up in Christian life from time to time. Christian life is a permanent conversion, but illumined and characterized in its very essence by the fact that God is our Father, by the consoling truth that "Our Lord is such a good Father that he anticipates our desire to be forgiven and comes forward to us, opening his arms with his grace."[37]

Only we ourselves, by our pride, can impede the divine and human marvel of our joyous conversion. Pride impedes the first condition for repentance: recognizing our own sin.

For this reason, God's sons and daughters, if they are good children of their Father, fight to be humble. They fight for the sort of humility that is far removed from weakness of character; the sort of humility that is also filled, from its very roots, with divine filiation—knowing that we are children of a Father who is always waiting for us with his arms wide open.

37. St. Josemaría, *Christ Is Passing By*, 64.

December 14, 1994

"But the father said to his servants, 'Bring quickly the best robe, and put it on him; and put a ring on his hand, and shoes on his feet'" (Lk 15:22).

"What a great eve the world is!"[38]

What will heaven, the eternal feast day in Love, be, if it has an eve—this world—that holds so much wonder and greatness? That holds so many good people, like the father in the parable?

What will hell be, if it is the negation of a feast day with such a great eve?

How much this world is worth, which is the preparation of that great, everlasting feast day! It stimulates us to make every second vibrant with eternity.

We can't do this alone, and so we say again and again, "Lord, with your grace; My Mother, with your help!" Until the aspiration "Thy face, Lord, do I seek" of Psalm 28 is fulfilled in the eternal "now" of glory.

---

38. Pedro Salinas, *La voz a ti debida*, Alianza, 1933, line 425.

65. A Great Feast

June 14, 2019

"Bring the fatted calf and kill it, and let us eat and make merry" (Lk 15:23).

Although our joy will not be expressed in the same way in every moment and circumstance, we should always be happy, both when we experience what is humanly pleasant and also when we confront suffering.

When we stay with Jesus, he says to all of us, as he said to his apostles, ". . . that my joy be in you" (Jn 15:11). And St. Paul exhorts us, "Rejoice in the Lord always; again I will say, Rejoice" (Phil 4:4).

The experience of our own weakness and our sins shouldn't make us fall into sadness either, because, as happened to the Prodigal Son (see Lk 15:22–24), genuine happiness is born of the certainty that we are always infinitely loved by God, who prepares a "great feast" for us every time we repent.

In this way we can always be, with Jesus, sowers of peace and joy.

66. Adopted and Raised Up

January 12, 1992

"See what love the Father has given us, that we should be called children of God; and so we are!" (1 Jn 3:1).

God, in an outpouring of goodness, not only wants us to treat him as our father, but in an incomparably greater outpouring of his love, he makes us his children in the strict sense, although a limited and partial one, by participation in the unique divine sonship in the full sense, of the Second Person of the Blessed Trinity. This membership of God's family is not, for us, simply a moral matter, about the way we behave. It is based on a real transformation, being raised to a higher order, being adopted as children. When we know and in some way experience this divine reality of our divinization, what stands out strongly is the fact that it is a free gift, which is built upon our weakness.

Being members of God's family is not something we achieve for ourselves, nor is it a further step along the path of human progress. It is a gift.

67. Our Way of Praying

August 10, 2019

"He told them a parable, to the effect that they ought always to pray and not lose heart" (Lk 18:1).

How often we have meditated on this necessity!

"One of his disciples said to him, 'Lord, teach us to pray, as John taught his disciples.' And he said to them, 'When you pray, say: "Father, . . .""" (Lk 11:1–2). Jesus started his own prayer by turning to his Father: with praise and thanksgiving (see Mt 11:25–26, Jn 11:41); at the Last Supper (see Jn 17:5); in Gethsemane (see Lk 22:42); and on the Cross (see Lk 23:34).

In union with Jesus Christ—through him and in him—we reach God the Father (see Jn 14:6), with simplicity, sincerity, and trust in his omnipotent love.

To take up a life of prayer every day is to allow ourselves to be accompanied, in the good moments and the bad, by the Person who best knows and loves us. Our dialogue with Jesus Christ opens up new perspectives for us, new ways of seeing things, that are always more filled with hope.

Let's ask the Holy Spirit to constantly renew the way we pray. The initiative is his: "the living and true God tirelessly calls each person to that mysterious encounter known as prayer."[39]

---

39. *Catechism of the Catholic Church*, 2567.

March 30, 2019

"Two men went up into the temple to pray" (Lk 18:10).

The Pharisee gave God thanks . . . apparently.

Recognizing that our own good qualities and good deeds would not be possible without help from heaven is something very good and necessary. But in reality, the Pharisee was praising himself, and above all he was despising others. He lacked something essential: a recognition that he too needed mercy and forgiveness.

In contrast, the publican, simply by confessing that he was a sinner and needed God's mercy, was forgiven.

When Our Lord ended the parable, he concluded, "Every one who exalts himself will be humbled, but he who humbles himself will be exalted."

God does not take pleasure in our humiliation; he wants our humility so that he can exalt us, so that, by emptying ourselves of our disordered self-love, we will open up a space in our lives to the action of his grace, his love. Prayer is humble.

69. The Last Place

June 22, 1977

"Every one who exalts himself will be humbled, but he who humbles himself will be exalted" (Lk 18:14).

It isn't usually difficult to put ourselves in the last place. But when we are put in the last place by others—or think we are, because sometimes it's only our imagination—maybe our pride rebels. At such times we understand more clearly why St. Josemaría said, "You're not humble when you humble yourself, but when you are humbled by others and you bear it for Christ."[40]

If we were truly humble, we would find it natural to be held in low esteem by other people. But the path to humility is a long one, lasting a lifetime. So at least when we notice our wounded pride rebelling like that, we can offer to Our Lord our desire to bear it without complaining even internally, but with a smile, with the underlying joy of a Christian soul. And it will be a good opportunity to pray through Our Lady, the handmaid of the Lord, "Jesus, make me humble yourself, because I'm proud."

Another step on the stairway of humility is to hide and disappear, when Our Lord permits us to get what we think of as a good result in our work, our apostolate, or any other aspect of our lives. Then we can let Jesus alone shine out, let God alone take the credit that is due to him.

In order to hide like this, it is not enough just to wait passively. Unless we practice, when the opportunity comes we won't manage to do it—we won't let ourselves be hidden. Sometimes we need to hide voluntarily by seeking to be the last. Otherwise, when we're put in last place by someone else,

40. St. Josemaría, *The Way*, 594.

we won't be able to stay there, in the background, as though we belonged there.

Hiding means not imposing our own judgments; listening to others with interest; when we can choose, letting others have the best of anything; avoiding praise for ourselves; wanting not to be praised; not claiming "rights" that are not really rights; avoiding many of the complaints that rise to our lips in the course of the day, so that only God knows the sacrifice a particular action costs us; not making it obvious how hard we work; and not talking about the personal effort that lay behind some notable achievement.

70. Questions for Young People
January 26, 2019

"Good Teacher, what must I do to inherit eternal life?" (Mk 10:17).

"When I look at thy heavens, the work of thy fingers, the moon and the stars which thou hast established; what is man that thou art mindful of him, and the son of man that thou dost care for him?" (Ps 8:3–4). These words of the Psalmist reflect the wonder that awakens in our souls when we contemplate the immensity of the universe and at the same time discover that in spite of our own littleness, we are loved unconditionally by God, as we are, for ourselves.

We may sometimes have the sensation that this experience of fulfilment is admirable, beautiful, but unachievable. We feel immersed in the whirlpool of life, crowded with tasks, projects, things that need doing. Then doubts may arise within us: "What is all this for? What is the meaning in my doing this or that? Where am I trying to get to? What do I really want?" These questions awaken in our soul because we aspire to something higher, and with the help of the Holy Spirit, they open us up to wider horizons.

Youth is an especially good time to ask ourselves these questions, because it is a time filled with possibilities, great challenges, and decisions that will mark the direction our life takes. Accordingly we need to have space, and time, for reflection, for allowing ideas to ripen and bear fruit, for thinking over what we have experienced up until now, so as to rediscover the present—what we each are—and plan for the future.

Behind these great questions, God wants to open up to us a panorama of greatness and beauty which may be hidden from our eyes. We need to trust in him and take a step toward an encounter with him.

God's plans for us are not to kill dreams but to kindle desires, to make our lives fruitful, so we can bring many smiles to people's lips and make many hearts dance. Pope Francis said this in his video message for the World Youth Day in Panama, thinking of the example of the Blessed Virgin Mary, who with her generous "Yes!" to God, changed the course of history forever.[41]

41. Pope Francis, *Video Message of his Holiness Pope Francis to Young People on the Occasion of the 34th World Youth Day 2019*, Panama, January 22 - 27, 2019, http:// www.vatican.va/content/francesco/en/messages/youth/documents/papa-francesco_20181121_videomessaggio-panama-gmg.html

71. Taking a Risk

November 1, 2019

"At that saying his countenance fell, and he went away sorrowful; for he had great possessions" (Mk 10:22).

Our Lord wants to give all his friendship to the rich young man, and offers him a panorama of happiness. But the young man prefers to take a different path.

Genuinely offering our friendship entails being willing to take a risk, since there is always a possibility that it may not be returned.

This is something Our Lord experiences in his own life: with that young man, or when, coming down from the Mount of Olives, he weeps over Jerusalem at the thought of those whose hearts are hardened (see Lk 19:41).

After experiences like that, which will arise sooner or later, we have to overcome the fear of taking that risk again, just as Jesus also does with each of us.

We need to accept our own vulnerability, to keep taking the first step without expecting anything in return, with our eyes on the great good that may come into being: a genuine friendship.

72. The Good of God

March 22, 1984

"You shall love the Lord your God . . ." (Mt 22:37).

Loving has many aspects . . . but what does loving God mean? Loving God means wanting to possess him, see him, rejoice in his infinite goodness: loving God means seeking union with him.

But that's not the whole of it; it's not the fullness of love.

The fullness of love—love of benevolence—means wanting the good of the beloved, and aiming to bring it about.

Can I bring God any good that he won't have unless I provide it? Yes: my own happiness (holiness) and that of others. It is part of the mystery of God in revealing himself to the world, and especially to free beings: God chose to create free beings because, humanly speaking, he wanted there to be people who would love him in the full sense, by bringing about God's good, or in other words God's glory, when the person giving glory to God is free. And that glory or good of God, which we can give him or refuse him, is our own happiness (and that of others), which means our union with him.

Thus, in respect to God, our "love of concupiscence" becomes our "love of benevolence." God, freely, has chosen to need us.

And by contrast, we see sin more clearly as an offense against God, and we understand more deeply the reality of atonement: it means being able to console God.

73. The Good of Our Neighbor

March 22, 1984

"... You shall love your neighbor as yourself" (Mt 22:39).

To love others for God's sake is to love God in them. "Truly, I say to you, as you did it to one of the least of these my brethren, you did it to me" (Mt 25:40).

Because charity—love for God and other people—is one single virtue, not two virtues.

The measure of our love and service to God is our love and service to others; not because other people are God, but because God loves them, desires their good, "needs" their good.

74. Patience and Impatience

February 26, 1999

"Love is patient" (1 Cor 13:4).

There are times when we feel impatience surging up: unexpected interruptions in our work, being kept waiting, the small or big setbacks of every day.

Let's think about—talk to!—Jesus straight away, saying, "You have more patience with me, Jesus."

Impatience, beyond what is instinctive, is a lack of interior mortification, and at base, a lack of charity.

Its opposites—understanding, forgiveness, peacefulness—are the outcome of real affection for God and other people. At the first stirring of impatience, let's try and smile at and pray for the person who is interrupting us, keeping us waiting, or tiring us at a given moment, and offer it up to Our Lord cheerfully.

The effort to smile when things go wrong is also an act of faith, an act of hope, and an act of charity.

Faith in God's loving, constant providence.

Hope in the saving effectiveness of the Cross.

Charity, because it means giving joy to others.

Jesus, with your grace; My Mother, with your help!

"By your endurance you will gain your lives" (Lk 21:19).

75. Everyone's Brothers and Sisters

April 4, 1992

"There is neither Jew nor Greek, there is neither slave nor free, there is neither male nor female; for you are all one in Christ Jesus" (Gal 3:28).

If people are children of the same father, they are consequently each other's brothers and sisters.

If we are God's children, we are brothers and sisters of one another, and the reality of our filiation brings a similar reality to our fraternity. The fact that we are children of God in Christ confers precise supernatural characteristics on Christian fraternity.

This fraternity is unity: we are all one in Christ. In the light of the mystery of the communion of saints, the Mystical Body of Christ, fraternity among Christians is not horizontal but vertical, in Christ.

The reality of our being brothers and sisters of all Christians is something much deeper, a much stronger bond, than the simple fraternity that derives from our shared human nature—it far surpasses the universal brotherhood of mankind, important though that is.

In a mystical but real way, we Christians, rather than being many brothers and sisters, are all one in Christ Jesus.

76. Love Steps Forward

April 4, 1977

"I have earnestly desired to eat this Passover with you before I suffer" (Lk 22:15).

"Before I suffer." Our Lord, because of his love for us, brings forward his sacrifice: the Mass, the Eucharist, is the sacramental actualization of the sacrifice of the Cross, where Jesus, with arms outstretched, gives his life for mankind.

From a purely human point of view it could seem more logical to institute the Eucharist after the Passion, death, and Resurrection. But love surpasses our reasoning; it doesn't wait for the time we would think better or more suitable. At any rate, that is what God's love is like: in the human heart of Jesus it anticipates things, brings them forward, instead of waiting for the time we would judge most "reasonable."

What is our love like? We will never be able to overtake Our Lord, because our love is always a response, today and now, to his. But Jesus tells us, in his New Commandment, "love one another as I have loved you" (Jn 15:12).

Christ's words "as I have loved you" invite us to step forward to love others. To love as Christ loves, our self-giving and service to the people around us have to bring things forward, not just wait for what is acceptable or reasonable—"when I can," "when they say so," or "if I'm asked."

By looking at Christ we will discover ways of acting sooner, without waiting to be asked for that act of love, that service, that sacrifice. We will bear one another's burdens, anticipating their needs in self-giving, like so many mothers and fathers who, through their disinterested service of their children, create broad spaces for friendship that spread far beyond their own family.

"And so fulfil the law of Christ" (Gal 6:2): we will not then believe ourselves to be heroic because we will only have fulfilled our duty, the law of Christ, which, as it commands us to love, is "the perfect law, the law of liberty" (Jas 1:25).

77. To the End

April 13, 2017

"Before the feast of the Passover, when Jesus knew that his hour had come to depart out of this world to the Father, having loved his own who were in the world, he loved them to the end" (Jn 13:1).

Let's go in our imagination to the Cenacle, the Upper Room, in Jerusalem, to contemplate the great proof of love Our Lord gives us: instituting the Blessed Eucharist.

Our God is always close to us. But in the Eucharist he comes especially close to our heart: Body, Blood, Soul, and Divinity.

Jesus loved us "to the end." Nobody is excluded from that love. For every single person, the Son of God became man, like us in everything "yet without sinning" (Heb 4:15). Still more, he chose to take on himself the sins of all mankind, to atone for them and restore us to friendship with God the Father.

There are many ways we can show our response to God's love. One way is to thank him for so much love by properly preparing to receive the sacrament of penance, to attend Mass and to receive Holy Communion.

Taking part in the Eucharistic Sacrifice is not just remembering Our Lord's self-giving for us. The Mass is much more: it is the actualization of the sacrifice of Calvary that was anticipated at the Last Supper.

St. John Paul II wrote that the sacrifice of the Cross "is so decisive for the salvation of the human race that Jesus Christ offered it and returned to the Father only after he had left us a means of sharing in it as if we had been present there."[42]

Thank you, Lord, for the Eucharist. And thank you for

---

42. St. John Paul II, *Ecclesia de Eucharistia*, Rome, April 17, 2003, 11.

faith, our faith, in the Eucharist. Thank you for the priesthood, which has perpetuated that love of yours in time. "God's love for his creatures is so boundless and our response to it should be so great that, when Holy Mass is being said, time ought to stand still."[43]

43. St. Josemaría, *The Forge*, 436.

78. Being Loved by God

November 13, 1979

"A new commandment I give to you, that you love one another; even as I have loved you" (Jn 13:34).

How enlightening it is to consider these words from the Second Vatican Council: "Man is the only creature on earth which God willed for itself"![44]

Still more: God, today and now and always, loves every single person for him or herself.

He wants their good, their full happiness, which is only found in God.

Human beings are not a means to an end. People cannot be treated as means for attaining something else, because God loves them for themselves. That is an absolute principle which shows the personal dignity of the human being. We can't use anyone as means to obtain a selfish end; but neither can they be used as means to achieve good or holy ends.

To treat someone as a means is to strip them of their personhood (to stop loving them for themselves) and turn them into an object (to love them for what we can get out of them, which is not love).

Love for God leads us to love other people for God's sake, and as God loves them; in other words, for themselves, not for our own benefit.

The New Commandment is always new, in the sense that we don't fulfil it completely; we never manage to love "as I have loved you," when the person speaking is infinite Charity, Love itself.

---

44. Second Vatican Council, Apostolic Constitution *Gaudium et spes*, 24.

79. True Concern

December 12, 1989

"By this all men will know that you are my disciples, if you have love for one another" (Jn 13:35).

Other people, everything to do with other people, must occupy my interest, concern, and time just as if it were my own affair. It is my own affair, because it is Christ's.

We need to concern ourselves with other people.

It's not enough just to occupy ourselves with doing things as they come up.

We have to anticipate others' needs, keep them in our thoughts, pray for them, and discover little ways of making life more pleasant for them.

"Even as I have loved you, that you also love one another" (Jn 13:34). Love goes still further: giving up our lives for others. Loving them to the end, with deeds.

80. Clothed in Christ

March 28, 1977

"And he took bread, and when he had given thanks he broke it and gave it to them, saying, 'This is my body which is given for you. Do this in remembrance of me'" (Lk 22:19).

Since then, the sublime action of Jesus Christ, that took place for the first time in the Upper Room at Jerusalem, has been repeated continually, in the Church, through her priests.

At the moment of the consecration during Mass, each priest is converted in a special way into *ipse Christus*, Christ himself.

Each priest lends Our Lord his voice, his hands, all his body, his will, his whole being. Those who attend Mass are also clothed in Christ, though in a different, analogous way.

How ought we to use our voice, our hands, our sight, our will, during the rest of the day, if Christ has made them his own in such a real way?

Whether we are priests or lay people, if we are clothed in Christ we make ourselves available like Our Lord, put ourselves at the service of others, and forget about our rights, for the sake of love.

Our smiles, the friendly way we treat people, are Christ's love for mankind. In our service to others, Jesus Christ's loving kindness toward every single person becomes visible.

The slightest unfaithfulness, the slightest lack of charity, ought to seem totally out of place to us. But as we are weak, we make ourselves children and appeal trustingly to Mary, as St. Josemaría did, using an aspiration inspired by the Letter to the Hebrews (Heb 4:16), in which Mary is called "the throne of grace." "Let us then with confidence draw near to the throne of grace, that we may receive mercy and find grace to help in time of need."

81. From Mass to Mass

March 5, 1998

"Drink of it, all of you; for this is my blood of the covenant" (Mt 26:27–28).

The contemplative life, a continuous reposing in God, is nourished primarily by Holy Mass and Eucharistic Communion, which is a foretaste of heaven and a pledge of eternal life: "He who eats my flesh and drinks my blood has eternal life, and I will raise him up at the last day" (Jn 6:54).

It would be beautiful, for each one of us, if our memory of the past centered on our last Mass, and our imagination about the future centered on our next Mass.

Consequently, not only would we avoid thinking unnecessarily about our own trifling concerns, but our examination of conscience and our resolutions would be more realistic and specific, directed toward the service of others, contemplating Jesus Christ's self-giving in the Eucharist.

82. He Calls the Poor

February 14, 2017

"When you give a feast, invite the poor, the maimed, the lame, the blind" (Lk 14:13).

We need Our Lord to enlarge our hearts, to give us hearts that suit him, so that all the needs, pains, and sufferings of the men and women of our time, especially the weakest, enter into it.

In today's world, poverty presents many faces: sick and elderly people treated with indifference, the loneliness felt by many abandoned people, the trauma of refugees, and the destitution in which a large part of mankind lives, often as a result of injustices that cry out to heaven.

None of this can leave us indifferent. Every Christian should put into action "the creativity of charity" that St. John Paul II talked about, in order to bring the balm of God's tenderness to all our brothers and sisters who are in need. "A friend of ours used to say: 'The poor are my best spiritual book and the main motive of my prayers. It pains me to see them, and in each one of them, Christ. And because it hurts, I realize I love him and love them.'"[45]

---

45. St. Josemaría, *Furrow*, 827.

83. Image of God

December 23, 1992

"I am in my Father, and you in me, and I in you" (Jn 14:20).

On seeing any picture or figure of Our Lord, whether in churches, people's homes, workplaces, the street, or museums, it is easy and natural for our soul to respond, with or without words, "Jesus, I love you."

But we should think that every person is an image of God. Let's pray, therefore, for the grace to learn to discover Jesus in other people, in each person, one by one.

As we see every person, we can say "My God, I love you," combining there, in an inseparable ideal, love for God and love for that brother or sister.

Seeing Our Lord in another can also become a prayer, a petition, that that person may come progressively closer to God, and become happier.

84. Our Life

February 13, 1992

"Jesus answered him, 'If a man loves me, he will keep my word, and my Father will love him, and we will come to him and make our home with him'" (Jn 14:23).

The path that gives us entry into the intimacy of the Father, the Son, and the Holy Spirit is to follow Christ, but in such a way that we not only imitate him but end up by becoming identified with him.

We are not children of the Father each on our own, so to speak, but we are children of the Father because we are Christ, without ceasing to be ourselves.

Through grace and the fact of being children of God, Christ's life is our life. "That is why a Christian should live as Christ lived, making the affections of Christ his own, so that he can exclaim with St. Paul: 'It is now no longer I that live, but Christ lives in me.'"[46]

This speaks to us of our effort to imitate Jesus, not as merely achieving a simple external resemblance, but as a result of the fact that he is living in us, in his distinct unity with the Father, as only begotten Son.

And in that spiritual union of us with him, by which we share in his divine sonship, we are, in him, children of the Father.

All this is a free gift from God, but a gift that requires a response on our part—our love, fulfilling his will, his words, his commandments.

---

46. See St. Josemaría, *Christ Is Passing By*, 103.

85. Peace and Uncertainty

March 20, 2014

"Peace I leave with you; my peace I give to you; not as the world gives do I give to you" (Jn 14:27).

We usually think of peace in terms of stability in our personal, professional, and social life; in families, a hopeful future for the children; good health; freedom from money worries; knowing that someone will look after us lovingly when we are old; and dreams coming true for ourselves and people we love. Basically what brings peace is loving and being loved.

God wants all that for us; he wants us to be happy.

However, life seems to consist of hoping for something that we never fully obtain. It is full of plans that are fulfilled and others that fail, happiness and suffering, health and sickness. This experience of inevitable limitations shows that from its very origin, mankind has been afflicted by a fundamental wound. Jesus, the Son of God, becomes incarnate and enters into this wound. He is born away from his home, he suffers slander from his own relations, suspicion by the authorities, sadness, and a violent death . . .

We can ask Jesus, "Have your dreams, your heart's desire, been fulfilled?" His dream was—and still is, because he lives for us—to save us by love, by making us capable of loving as he loves. "He is our peace" (Eph 2:14).

When we love the Cross we discover that, in that interweaving of joys and sorrows, we can always open ourselves to God and other people. We will recover peace when confronted by difficulties and problems, if we cease to be the center of our own affection and attention.

Amidst the suffering of the Cross, Jesus continues loving.

He asks his Father to forgive his executioners, he does not forget his Mother or St. John, he responds to the Good Thief . . . Love is what has brought him to the Cross, love for every single one of us.

"Not as the world gives do I give to you . . ."

86. Transmitting Peace

March 20, 2014

"Peace I leave with you" (Jn 14:27).

God wants each of us to have peace in ourselves and to pass it on to others. "You've written to me and I quote: 'My joy and my peace. I can never have real happiness if I don't have peace. And what is peace? Peace is something closely related to war. Peace is a consequence of victory. Peace demands of me a continuous struggle. Without struggle I won't be able to have peace.'"[47]

In our interior struggle God is asking us for our responses, and with his help we activate our freedom to love. The more, and the more freely, we love, the more peace we have within us, regardless of our personal circumstances and the situation around us. Hence our struggle is not restlessness or lack of serenity.

When we have peace we pass it on to others by our presence, by the way we react to people and events. Christ, the "Prince of Peace" (Is 9:6), enables us to see through his eyes. Being "sowers of peace and joy with what we say and what we do,"[48] as St. Josemaría wrote, is the sign of Christians, their inner attitude in relating to others and passing on the Gospel.

47. St. Josemaría, *The Way*, 308.
48. St. Josemaría, *Christ Is Passing By*, 168.

87. Uncomplicated

February 17, 2016

"Let not your hearts be troubled, neither let them be afraid" (Jn 14:27).

Interior mortification is necessary and sometimes acquires higher value than other kinds of penance that may look more difficult.

Among its many aspects, an important one is not to keep thinking about our own faults, possible personal difficulties, or sins, outside the right time for doing so—the sacrament of penance and our examination of conscience . . .

At the other extreme, we should ask Our Lord to help us not to consider our own faults inevitable. That can happen when we find that we keep repeating the same errors, even in something small such as distractions in prayer.

Maybe we don't consider them inevitable in theory, but in practice we do, when our struggle not to get distracted is always the same. Then we fail to look for ways to fight them more effectively, above all by asking for help from heaven when we start.

The peace of Jesus prevents all inner complication, and at the same time it impels us to undertake a serene struggle for love, which we are always able to renew.

88. No Distinctions

April 8, 1992

"As the Father has loved me, so have I loved you" (Jn 15:9).

There are countless ways we should practice fraternity in ordinary life. But the root from which they all spring is none other than the fact that we are God's children.

"We have to behave as God's children toward all God's sons and daughters,"[49] is how St. Josemaría summed up the demands of fraternal charity rooted in our divine filiation. This supernatural foundation means that fraternity among Christians must include respect, which is not coldness or officiousness, but which endows it, on the human plane, with good manners; love and respect for others is love and respect for the image of Christ, for Christ himself in them.

As well as that supernatural fraternity stemming from the grace of God, we should extend to everyone the fraternity that stems from us all being created by God, and called to the warmth of our Father's household.

Over and above any differences, we Christians should always bear in mind that "Our Lord has come to bring peace, the good news, life, to all men. Not only to the rich, or only to the poor. Not only to the wise, or only to the simple. To everyone. To brothers, for brothers we are, because we are children of the same Father, God. So, there is but one race: the race of the children of God. There is but one color: the color of the children of God. And there is but one language: that which speaks to the heart and to the head, without the noise of words, but giving us knowledge of God and making us love one another."[50]

---

49. St. Josemaría, *Christ Is Passing By*, 36.
50. St. Josemaría, *Christ Is Passing By*, 106.

89. Innovating Love

March 16, 2000

"Abide in my love" (Jn 15:9).

"Sing to the Lord a new song!" exhorts Psalm 98.

Every day as it begins should really be the beginning of a new song, because of the newness of our love.

The newness of our struggle, just as yesterday, in the newness of love, today and now.

Lord, we can't sing that new song unless you set the pitch, unless you sustain the notes, unless you whisper the words in our ears.

We don't need to "invent" resolutions, but to invent love in the usual, everyday things.

90. What We Find Hard

January 9, 2018

"These things I have spoken to you, that my joy may be in you, and that your joy may be full" (Jn 15:11).

In speaking to his apostles, Jesus is also speaking to us. He wants joy, happiness, to fill all of us, and to fill everything in our lives. He wants us to be happy even in times of suffering, which will inevitably come.

Therefore we need to ask ourselves how we can joyfully carry out even duties that we may find unpleasant.

Let's consider this: "we shouldn't think that the only work we can do joyfully is what we find pleasing."[51] We can carry out joyfully—and not reluctantly—what we find hard, what doesn't please us, if we do it for and with love and, therefore, freely.

When saying his prayer aloud, on April 28, 1963, St. Josemaría spoke about the lights God had granted him years before in 1931: "You have led me to understand, Lord, that having the Cross means finding happiness, joy. And the reason, as I now see more clearly than ever, is this: having the Cross means being identified with Christ, being Christ, and therefore being a child of God."[52]

Looking at Jesus on the Cross is, paradoxically, a direct path to happiness, to the happiness that he wants for us, and that he wants to be full.

51. St. Josemaría, Letter dated December 29, 1947—February 14, 1966, 106.
52. St. Josemaría, Notes taken from a meditation, April 28, 1963.

91. The Joy of God's Children

May 1, 1992

"These things I have spoken to you, … that your joy may be full" (Jn 15:11).

Possessing the good, and the hope of possessing it, produces the state of soul that we call joy.

Our joy may stem from the possession of an ephemeral, passing good or the eternal good; and it may be just on the surface of the soul or go to its very depths.

There are many contingent joys which are necessarily passing; there is also laughter that masks sadness, and there are tears of joy . . .

In this life there can be no fuller joy than that of God's children, because no good can compare with the infinite riches of being members of God's family, children of God; nothing in this world ought to rob us of our joy.

This joy is sure hope, serenity, cheerfulness, which is not the "cheerfulness of a healthy animal," but that "of knowing that our Father God loves us with preferential love, that he welcomes us, helps us, and forgives us."[53]

This joy is not based on our virtues; it is not vain self-satisfaction, but is built on our human weakness and fragility.

Knowing our own weakness, experiencing the presence of conflict within ourselves, can and should give way to joy.

---

53. St. Josemaría, *The Way*, 659, and *The Forge*, 332.

92. Newness

April 13, 2017

"That you love one another as I have loved you" (Jn 15:12).

Jesus gave us this express command at the Last Supper. And to engrave it on his disciples' memory, and on ours, he washed his apostles' feet.

St. John wrote in his first letter, "By this we know love, that he laid down his life for us; and we ought to lay down our lives for the brethren" (1 Jn 3:16).

How will we do that? There are many ways of putting Our Lord's New Commandment into practice. Forgiving, excusing, understanding, taking a sincere interest in other people, performing little acts of service in daily life in the family, at work, at leisure, and so on; all these are opportunities of bringing Our Lord's commandment to life, making it part of our own lives.

At the Last Supper Jesus also prayed to the Father for the unity of those who would be called by him down through the centuries. ". . . [T]hat they may all be one; even as thou, Father, art in me, and I in thee, that they also may be in us, so that the world may believe that thou hast sent me" (Jn 17:21). Let's try to be instruments of unity wherever we are.

Even as thou, Father, art in me, and I in thee. We are to share in the union of the Three Persons of the Blessed Trinity: in the Holy Spirit, infinite Love. True unity among everyone is the fruit of love.

May Our Lady, Mother of Fair Love, obtain for us by her motherly mediation the grace of more intense faith in God's love for us and greater charity toward other people.

November 1, 2019

"No longer do I call you servants, for the servant does not know what his master is doing; but I have called you friends" (Jn 15:15).

At the start of the new millennium, St. John Paul II said that all the apostolic initiatives that arise in the future will become "mechanisms without a soul" if they are not grounded on a sincere love for every person, on being "able to share their joys and sufferings, to sense their desires and attend to their needs, to offer them deep and genuine friendship."[54]

Friendship multiplies joys and offers comfort in sorrows. A Christian's friendship desires the greatest happiness—a relationship with Jesus Christ—for those close to him or her.

What a wonderful prayer St. Josemaría offered: "Give us, Jesus, hearts to the measure of yours!" That is the path to giving "soul" to the apostolate, and bringing that full happiness to our home, our work, and every place we find ourselves.

---

54. St. John Paul II, Apostolic Letter *Novo Millennio Ineunte*, Rome, January 6, 2001, 43.

94. The World Will Hate You
March 7, 2018

"If the world hates you, know that it has hated me before it hated you" (Jn 15:18).

We love the world, created by God and regenerated by Christ, but we also find things in the world that are opposed to Jesus Christ, about which St. John says, "Do not love the world or the things in the world" (1 Jn 2:15). This is the "triple concupiscence," which does not come from God (see 1 Jn 2:16).

Many Christians live in surroundings that are indifferent to God. In other places they are attacked and persecuted. The rejection of God and of people who follow him runs through history, because "A disciple is not above his teacher" (Mt 10:24).

The *Acts of the Apostles* is a book punctuated by violence, from St. Stephen's stoning to the beginnings of St. Paul's martyrdom. But the superabundant love for God of its main characters overcomes the violence, so that it is not the outstanding feature of the narrative. Instead, the book is centered on the Holy Spirit, infinite Love, and the spreading of the Faith.

We too have to understand and share the yearnings of our time, discover what is positive, evaluate and contribute to material progress, and share people's desires for justice and freedom. Today, as then, "'Behold, the days are coming,' says the Lord God, 'when I will send a famine on the land; not a famine of bread, nor a thirst for water, but of hearing the words of the Lord'" (Am 8:11).

In our ambition to bring the joy of the Gospel to everyone, we will meet setbacks, and like Jesus' first followers, we wish to love not only what is good and beautiful in the world but also the people who are indifferent or opposed to Jesus Christ. We want to act with mercy and forgiveness, not judging people. Despite our personal weakness we will try to follow what St. Paul asks of us: "Do not be overcome by evil, but overcome evil with good" (Rom 12:21).

95. Sensing Your Presence

March 10, 2004

"All mine is yours, and yours is mine" (Jn 17:10).

God's presence sustains everything: creation, conservation of being in me, in each other, in everything . . .

But St. Thomas Aquinas explains, "Grace is caused in man by the presence of the Godhead, as light in the air by the presence of the sun."[55]

The love of God transforms a person in such a way that they continue being the same person, but inundated with God. Hence Christian life is not merely a matter of moral or ethical improvement; it is identification with Christ, in a context of infinite love.

Lord, always be sun and light for me and for everyone!

---

55. St. Thomas Aquinas, *Summa Theologiae*, III, q. 7, a. 13.

96. Communion of Love

March 14, 2019

". . . [T]hat they may all be one; even as thou, Father, art in me, and I in thee, that they also may be in us, so that the world may believe that thou hast sent me" (Jn 17:21).

This is Our Lord's prayer for the unity of his future disciples.

May we all be one. This is not just the unity of a humanly well-structured organization but the unity that Love gives, "as you, Father, are in me, and I in you." The first Christians were a clear example of this: "the company of those who believed were of one heart and soul" (Acts 4:32).

Because it is the result of love, this unity is not uniformity but communion. It is unity in diversity, shown in being happy to live together with all our differences, learning to be enriched by others, nurturing an atmosphere of affection around us.

Jesus says that this unity is a condition for effectiveness in passing on the Gospel: "that the world may believe." Unity, therefore, does not create a closed group but opens us to offering our friendship to everyone, in a magnificent evangelizing mission.

97. Unity and Division
March 17 1990

". . . [T]hat they may become perfectly one, so that the world may know that thou hast sent me" (Jn 17:23).

A father, a mother, who loves two children madly, rejoices to see mutual affection between them and suffers if they see that the two don't have that affection.

"What were you discussing on the way?" Jesus asked them. "But they were silent; for on the way they had discussed with one another who was the greatest" (Mk 9:33–34).

How disappointed Jesus must have felt! Nevertheless he entrusted the Church to them, as he now entrusts her to us, who also fall into arguments and division.

Parents have a precious legacy to give their children: the example of their love for one another, which will be strong enough to overcome their children's selfishness too. An absence of love and forgiveness among their children is an open wound in parent's hearts.

Divisions between "good people" show that we are not really so good, and that unity needs God's permanent help and protection; it can't be taken for granted. Without unity, our charity lacks all credibility.

When we love others we are a source of joy for God and for Our Lady. This thought, which holds a very important truth, will spur us to put right any unloving reaction toward someone.

We possess the kingdom as the fruit of charity, now also as a foretaste, through giving ourselves to others as he gives himself to us.

104. Ecce Homo: A Vulnerable God

April 9, 2020

"Here is the man!" (Jn 19:5).

With these words Pilate, on the morning of Good Friday, presents Christ, tortured and humiliated, to the people.

Titian painted a famous work, the *Ecce Homo*—"here is the man!"—where the Innocent One, his Godhead hidden and reduced to ruin as a man, still allows his divinity and beauty to shine through.[60] God has chosen to make himself visible even in his vulnerability. In the darkness that so often accompanies suffering, let us seek light in Jesus, who suffers and who says, "I am the light of the world" (Jn 8:12).

St. John Paul II exclaimed, "It is man, every man, every man in his unique, unrepeatable being, created and redeemed by God . . . *Ecce Homo!*" Although we may have people with us, in the final analysis, each person experiences suffering alone with God. The loneliness of Jesus—*Ecce Homo!*—also reminds us of those who have no one to love them in sickness, old age, and death. Jesus, rejected by all, also experienced that loneliness. His cry on the Cross—"Why have you abandoned me?"—maybe began earlier, in his serene silence at the scene of the *Ecce Homo*.

The figure of Christ Pilate presented to the people is also an icon of mistreated human dignity. There is a mysterious presence of God in every person's suffering—not only when we are innocent, but even when our sufferings are caused by our sins. We ask God to help us, to save us. Christ in his Passion has taken upon himself all the consequences of people's sins.

A special presence of God is also found in those who give

---

60. See Titian (Tiziano Vecellio), *Ecce Homo* (1547), oil on slate, Museo del Prado.

themselves to others disinterestedly, because "where there is charity and love, there God is present. *Ubi caritas et amor, Deus ibi est!*"[61] So many women and men go beyond the call of duty in their service at work, in families, in ordinary life, like Good Samaritans.

Titian, after painting the *Ecce Homo*, painted the *Mater Dolorosa with Open Hands*.[62] For many years, the two paintings hung side by side on the same wall. When suffering enters our lives, may we also realize, as we look at Jesus, vulnerable, "Light from Light," that we are always accompanied by Mary.

61. Hymn *Ubi Caritas*.
62. See Titian (Tiziano Vecellio), *Mater Dolorosa with Open Hands* (1555), oil on marble, Museo del Prado.

105. Filling the World with Kindness

February 5, 2020

"Daughters of Jerusalem, do not weep for me, but weep for yourselves and for your children" (Lk 23:28).

Jesus Christ was "born of a woman" (Gal 4:4); this same woman, the Virgin Mary, out of her ardent zeal to serve others, advanced the hour of her Son's public activity at Cana (see Jn 2:4–5).

At the time of Jesus' abandonment, it was the "daughters of Jerusalem" (Lk 23:28) who forced their way through the crowd to accompany him; women were standing at the foot of the Cross when our redemption was being carried out (see Jn 19:25); and a woman was the first witness to Our Lord's Resurrection (see Jn 20:16), to the Good News that afterwards would spread to every nation.

On the holiness of women depends, in large part, the holiness of the people around them. Let us turn our eyes to the Gospel once more, and ask Jesus to grant us the faith and trust of our Mother and the holy women, and the ability to produce virtuous circles around us that will fill the world of work, civil society, and families with kindness.

106. Cross and Paradise

March 30, 2018

"Crucify him, crucify him!" (Jn 19:6).

After being scourged and crowned with thorns, Jesus carries his Cross, in the presence of the people he loves; he is stripped of his garments, and, apparently, of his dignity too. At the moment of the crucifixion, Our Lord addresses these words to God the Father, as reported by St. Matthew: "My God, my God, why hast thou forsaken me?" (Mt 27:46; see Mk 15:34).

We might wonder, why all this suffering? Why the Cross?

Although we cannot understand it completely, the Crucifixion reveals to us that right where there seems to be nothing but weakness, God shows his limitless power. Where we see failure, defeat, incomprehension, and hatred, precisely there Jesus reveals to us God's great power, the power that transforms the Cross into an expression of Love.

That is the experience of the "Good Thief" on Golgotha: at the moment of total failure and weakness, he experiences how the Cross of Jesus becomes the place of power, where he knows that he is forgiven and loved: "Today you will be with me in Paradise," Our Lord tells him (Lk 23:43).

Cross and paradise. This is the Christian paradox: on the Cross we hear the word "paradise" spoken. From being an instrument of torture, violence, and disgrace, the Cross is transformed into a means of salvation, a symbol of hope. It has become a sign of God's freely-given, merciful love, which becomes present for us, in an eminently effective way, in the Blessed Eucharist and the other sacraments.

To look at the Crucified One is to contemplate our hope. To adore the Holy Cross is an act of faith and a proclamation of Jesus' victory.

107. Suffering and Clarity

September 9, 2019

"Standing by the cross of Jesus were his mother, and his mother's sister, Mary the wife of Clopas, and Mary Magdalene" (Jn 19:25).

In conversations with a great variety of people, spontaneous remarks sometimes come up about situations that are difficult, cause suffering, or leave us in interior darkness. On these occasions, words of St. Josemaría about the Mother of Jesus often come to mind. God wished to raise Our Lady up with the fullness of grace, but "it is equally true that he did not spare her pain, exhaustion in her work, or trials of her faith."[63]

Although we will never fully understand this, if we look at Mary, above all at the foot of the Cross, it will help us understand a bit more of the experience of suffering. And we will discover little by little the meaning of St. Paul's words: "In my flesh I complete what is lacking in Christ's afflictions for the sake of his body, that is, the Church" (Col 1:24). Thus suffering can become a place where we find clarity, peace, and even joy: light, rest, happiness in the Cross.

/

63. St. Josemaría, *Christ Is Passing By*, 172.

108. Children with Mary and Joseph

March 13, 1992

"Then he said to the disciple, 'Behold, your mother!' And from that hour the disciple took her to his own home" (Jn 19:27).

We only need to think about Our Lady's role in the work of our salvation, and her incomparable union with God, to try and learn from her how to respond fully to God's action, which makes us too into members of the family of God the Father, Son, and Holy Spirit.

She is our mother insofar as we are children of God, brothers and sisters of Christ. Having God for our Father, at the same time we have Our Lady for our mother, as Jesus told us on the Cross.

God is the one cause of our grace and our supernatural adoption, but he has chosen that all his graces should come to us through Mary's motherly mediation.

And together with Mary, by God's will, is Joseph, who took the place of a father to Jesus and in some way also acts as father to those who want to identify themselves with Christ: to the children of God.

St. Joseph "really is a father and lord. He protects those who revere him and accompanies them on their journey through this life—just as he protected and accompanied Jesus when he was growing up." He is "also a teacher of interior life—for he teaches us to know Jesus and share our life with him, and to realize that we are part of God's family."[64]

When we behave as children toward Mary and Joseph, they lead us to Jesus, to live his life, to identify ourselves with him. And in Jesus, the Only-Begotten Son of the Father, we have

---

64. St. Josemaría, *Christ Is Passing By*, 39.

access to the divine intimacy of the Blessed Trinity.

April 9, 2019

"When Jesus had received the vinegar, he said, 'It is finished'; and he bowed his head and gave up his spirit" (Jn 19:30).

On Good Friday we contemplate in Christ crucified the immensity of his redeeming love. This love led him to be fully available and obedient to the will of God the Father.

Following Jesus and identifying with him also leads us, within our personal circumstances, to unlimited availability for the challenges and requirements of the Christian mission to bring the joy of the Gospel to everyone. In our daily life, we want to discover the voice of Christ who calls and invites us to broaden our horizons. Like St. Paul, we want to become "all things to all men" (1 Cor 9:22).

Let's look at the example of availability set by Guadalupe Ortiz de Landázuri,[65] whose life project was greatly expanded by placing herself within the divine plan. Guadalupe let herself be led by God, joyfully and spontaneously, from one place to another, from one job to another. Our Lord strengthened her abilities and talents, enriched her personality, and multiplied the fruitfulness of her life.

Despite our shortcomings and mistakes, God will also do great good for many people through us. He will do this by means of our availability to listen, serve, help, and let ourselves be helped: in short, to love whatever he wants. And, always and in everything, with the freedom and joy of the daughters and sons of God.

65. Guadalupe was beatified on May 18, 2019.

110. Consoling Christ and His Mother

February 20, 1980

"[Jesus] said, 'It is finished'; and he bowed his head and gave up his spirit" (Jn 19:30).

Sinners "crucify the Son of God on their own account and hold him up to contempt" (Heb 6:6).

Christ suffered for all the sins of mankind. His sacrifice on the Cross was superabundant. Through his own blood "he entered once for all into the Holy Place . . . thus securing an eternal redemption" (Heb 9:12).

Someone who remains in sin is in a way despising the fruits of the Passion, so that sinners, for their part, reopen the wounds of the Son of God. Now, today, we can think that Christ, glorious in heaven, and Our Lady, suffer for the sins people commit in the present, in a way that we cannot fully understand or explain.

Jesus and Mary possess eternal bliss and measureless happiness, but they know the today and now of sin on this earth, and it does not leave them indifferent. It is not just that they suffered two thousand years ago for those sins; now too, in some mysterious way, compatible with glory, they suffer. Sinners crucify Christ again, though not in time. It is maybe the Passion of Christ being offered spiritually for the sins committed today.

Our limited experience of time and its relation to eternity make it impossible for us to understand how this can be so, but it doesn't stop us from thinking about the mystery and acting accordingly.

Atonement is a present reality in us, and in Our Lord and Our Lady. Penance and expiation unite us to Christ on the Cross in the present, not only in the past.

Consoling Christ and his Mother Mary today and now is no pious metaphor but an urgent reality in this world that constantly renews the Passion of Christ. And this world includes me, you, each and every one of us.

But does our suffering console Our Lord? No. What consoles him is our love, our compassion. If at any point he wants us to have a cross, it is not because he wants our suffering, but because like that, with him, we are happier and can be more *ipse Christus*, Christ himself, children of God.

111. Christ in Other People

April 27, 1978

"You were bought with a price" (1 Cor 6:20).

Christ became incarnate and gave himself up on the Cross for each of us. We are worth his life, his self-surrender, his sacrifice.

We can each think, "I, in spite of my nothingness, am worth a great price: I'm worth all the Blood of Christ!"

We are instruments of great value, but we have to let ourselves be led docilely, by Jesus Christ.

And the same is true of other people: each soul is worth all the Blood of Christ!

Jesus, may nobody seem unimportant to us. Jesus, may other's problems not leave us indifferent. How much less those of my brothers and sisters, those of the people who live or work with me!

Some of us remember St. Josemaría asking, "Do you know why I love you so much?" And he supplied the answer: "Because I see the Blood of Christ running in your veins!"

That's the secret: seeing Jesus in our parents, our brothers and sisters, our friends, our coworkers, or classmates. Seeing Christ in the needy, the sick, those who are wounded in body or spirit, the unemployed, and those who have suffered a family disaster.

Holy Mary, show us Jesus in other people!

112. A New Light

April 1, 2018

"Mary Magdalene went and said to the disciples, 'I have seen the Lord!'"(Jn 20:18).

"The light of Christ!" The Church makes this proclamation ring out three times at the start of the Easter Vigil, announcing the truth that fills us with joy: the light of Christ opens up a path through the darkness of sin and death! Jesus has risen!

The darkness of Calvary is not the final word. The holy women, who accompanied Our Lord in his Passion, lead us toward the light of his Resurrection. Jesus rewards the love that moved them to want to embalm his body, and makes them the first bearers of the joy of Easter.

The news of the Resurrection offers us, like the holy women, new light. St. Paul reminds the Romans that we Christians are united to Our Lord's death "so that as Christ was raised from the dead by the glory of the Father, we too might walk in newness of life" (Rom 6:4).

We are not tied down by our past sins, which have been forgiven, or by the weight of our previous mistakes. Nor are we tied down by the limitations we can see in our lives. And so the Apostle Paul says again: "Consider yourselves dead to sin and alive to God in Christ Jesus" (Rom 6:11).

But what is the newness to which Our Lord is calling us? What does it consist of? It is the light of faith that illumines our lives, and that is enlivened by charity and sustained by hope.

113. There You Will See Him

April 1, 2018

"But go, tell his disciples and Peter that he is going before you to Galilee; there you will see him, as he told you" (Mk 16:7).

These are the angel's instructions to the holy women, after announcing Jesus' Resurrection to them.

The disciples are called to return to Galilee, to the place where everything began, to the land through which they had daily travelled with the Master during the years of his preaching.

The same call is addressed to us: to go back to our Galilee, to our daily life, but bringing to it the light and the joy of Easter.

Pope Francis reminded us of this a few years ago: "To return to Galilee means above all to return to that blazing light with which God's grace touched me at the start of the journey. From that flame I can light a fire for today and every day, and bring heat and light to my brothers and sisters."[66]

Let us receive the light Our Lord wants to give us, and share it with those around us. Like the holy women, let us joyfully announce the truth that Christ is alive.

To do so, let us turn to Our Lady's intercession, seeing her radiant with joy at her Son's Resurrection.

66. Pope Francis, Homily, Easter Vigil, Rome, April 19, 2014.

114. A Question from Our Lord

January 9, 2018

"Do you love me?" (Jn 21:17).

Christian life is a free response, imbued with initiative and availability, to Our Lord's question.

We can love because he has loved us first (see 1 Jn 4:10). Our faith in God's love for each one of us (see 1 Jn 4:16) leads us to respond fully, for love.

How liberating it is to know that God loves us! How liberating God's pardon is, that allows us to return to ourselves and to our true home (see Lk 15:17–24)!

It gives us a sense of security to know that God's infinite love is to be found not only at the origin of our existence, but also at every moment of our lives. For God is closer to us than we are to ourselves.[67]

Realizing that God is waiting for us in each person (see Mt 25:40), and that he wants to make himself present in their lives also, through us, makes us want to share what we have received abundantly with others.

In our lives, we have received and we still receive a lot of love. Giving love to God and to others is the truest act of freedom. "When a mother sacrifices herself for love of her children, she has made a choice, and the more she loves the greater will be her freedom."[68] Love fulfills freedom, it redeems it. Love enables freedom to discover its origin and goal, the Love of God.

---

67. See St. Augustine, *Confessions*, III, 6, 11.
68. St. Josemaría, *Friends of God*, 30.

115. Despoiled

February 25, 2010

"The Lord Jesus, after he had spoken to them, was taken up into heaven, and sat down at the right hand of God" (Mk 16:19).

Jesus took the form of a servant. Although his nature was divine, he "did not count equality with God a thing to be grasped, but emptied himself, taking the form of a servant, being born in the likeness of men" (Phil 2:6–7).

He despoiled himself totally of his right to be treated as God; from Bethlehem to the Cross.

And also afterwards: by his ascension, he stripped himself of the possibility of appearing, risen and glorious, in the Temple, before the Sanhedrin . . . his accusers.

This is the path for us to follow too. We can strip ourselves of our own ego, to live and rejoice through Christ, with Christ, and in Christ.

116. The Promise of the Spirit

June 4, 1995

"When the day of Pentecost had come... they were all filled with the Holy Spirit" (Acts 2:1, 4).

The Holy Spirit is sent down visibly: the great Gift, the Person who is the mutual love of God the Father and God the Son. A purifying fire, and a wind that bursts in impetuously: knowledge, love, and evangelizing zeal. The apostles, courageous, filled with wisdom, are now able to understand and pass on the Good News.

He is sent down invisibly: the Holy Spirit is the "sweet Guest of our souls."[69] He makes us children of God. "For all who are led by the Spirit of God are sons of God..., it is the Spirit himself bearing witness with our spirit that we are children of God" (Rom 8:14, 16). That witness is the filial love in our souls, which we want to rule the whole of our day: fire and rushing wind.

Pentecost is the beginning of the Church's journey among the nations, starting from Jerusalem. "Parthians and Medes and Elamites and residents of Mesopotamia . . ." (Acts 2:9), all mankind is summoned to receive the gift of the Risen Christ. The Church, visibly, is one people. With regard to her constitution, she is the Body of Christ; with regard to her operations, she is the sacrament of salvation. The Church is the People of God, suffused and united by the Holy Spirit, with the Pope as the visible principle of the unity of faith and communion.

The Church is also a collection of weak men and women, ourselves, who need to be constantly taught by the Holy Spirit. "The Counselor, the Holy Spirit, whom the Father will send

---

69. Mass of Pentecost Sunday, Sequence.

in my name, he will teach you all things, and bring to your remembrance all that I have said to you" (Jn 14:26).

He teaches us the truth about God, the world, others, and ourselves; the truth that sets us free (see Jn 8:32).

At Pentecost we find Mary: daughter of God the Father, mother of God the Son, spouse of God the Holy Spirit, mother of the newborn Church.

117. The Ultimate Reason

January 4, 1992

"So then you are no longer strangers and sojourners, but you are fellow citizens with the saints and members of the household of God" (Eph 2:19).

If we are looking for a deep, radical, realistic understanding of our life, the first thing we need to do is raise our eyes to heaven.

Only in God, in his global plan for our history, can we find the why and wherefore of our life. Not only because he created us, but because in addition, "we have been put here on earth for a further purpose: to enter into communion with God himself."[70]

Human nature as such possesses the consistency and dignity of having been created by God. However, the ultimate reason why God created it lies beyond itself.

God created us because he chose to, in order to give us, freely, a far higher dignity: that of being his children, of achieving the happiness of being *domestici Dei*, members of his household (see Eph 2:19).

He created us in such a way that we could be brought into the intimacy of his family, into the life of the Father, the Son, and the Holy Spirit, without destroying or forcing our own nature as created beings.

The mode of this adoption, brought about through sanctifying grace, is "divine filiation": we enter into communion with God by way of sonship, which in God is in fact the Only-Begotten Son of the Father.

---

70. St. Josemaría, *Christ Is Passing By*, 100.

118. Communion and Eternity

November 4, 2018

"We always thank God, the Father of Our Lord Jesus Christ, when we pray for you, because we have heard of your faith in Christ Jesus and of the love which you have for all the saints, because of the hope laid up for you in heaven" (Col 1:3–5).

Our hope is in heaven (see Col 1:5), a hope that illuminates our steps on earth. This hope tells us that the world in which we live will one day be transformed into "new heavens and a new earth" (2 Pt 3:13).

It also tells us that our daily activities have a meaning that goes beyond what we see directly around us. They become "vibrant with eternity" if we do them out of love for God and for others.

Another reality that fills us with consolation is the communion of saints. How much it encourages us to know that we are never alone, that in Christ we are one Body! We build up the Church wherever we are: all together and everywhere. We sustain one another!

119. Vessels of Clay

November 1, 2017

"What no eye has seen, nor ear heard, nor the heart of man conceived, what God has prepared for those who love him" (1 Cor 2:9).

On All Saints Day we celebrate that quiet and simple sanctity—sanctity without any human splendor—which seems to leave no trace in history, but shines forth before God. It leaves behind in the world a sowing of Love from which nothing is lost.

In thinking about so many men and women who have already traveled that path and now are rejoicing in God, I recalled some words of prayer by St. Josemaría: "I ask myself many times each day: what will it be like when all the beauty, all the goodness, all the infinite marvel of God is poured into this poor vessel of clay that I am, that we all are? . . . And then I understand what the Apostle said: 'eye has not seen, nor ear heard . . .' (1 Cor 2:9). It is worthwhile my children, it is worthwhile."[71]

We are poor vessels of clay: fragile, easily broken. But God has created us to fill us with his happiness, forever. And now, here on earth, he gives us his joy so that we may spread it to everyone.

Yes, it is possible to be happy amid uncertainty, problems, worries. St. Teresa of Calcutta said, "True love is a love that causes us pain, that hurts, and yet brings us joy."[72]

With our life and our prayer let us also accompany the deceased who, although they are suffering because their "vessel of clay" is not yet ready for all of God's beauty, already have the joy of knowing that he is waiting for them in heaven.

71. St. Josemaría, *Obras* 1966, pp. 8–9 (AGP, Biblioteca, P03).
72. St. Teresa of Calcutta, *No Greater Love*, New World Library, Novato CA, 2001, p.27.

Abandonment
  in God, 1, 32, 40, 42, 61, 99, 100
Angels, 5, 9, 20, 61, 113
Apostle, the, 19, 31, 54, 58
Apostolate
  speak about Christ, 11, 19
  personal, 19, 58
  and God's help, 19
  and mission, 34
  of friendship, 19, 35
  giving witness, 19
  and difficulties, 52
  and initiative, 58, 93
  and humility, 69
  and interior life, 93
Ascetical Struggle
  and youthful spirit, 29
  beginning again, 40, 61, 89
  and humility, 63
  and peace, 86
  and freedom, 86
  seeking God's help, 87, 89
  with God's grace, 40
Aspirations, suggested by St. Josemaría,
  apart from me you can do nothing, 54
  Domine, adauge nobis fidem, 1
  Domine, ut videam!, let me receive my sight, 3, 43
  Domine, ut videamus! Ut videant!, 4
  Gratias tibi, Deus, 41

If God is for us, who is against us, 1
Increase our faith!, 54, 55
Jesus, let's do this between the two of us, 6
Let us then with confidence draw near to the throne of
    grace, that we may receive mercy, 80
Lord, teach us to pray, 61, 67
May I see with your eyes, my Christ, 4
Omnes cum Petro ad Iesum per Mariam, 52
Omnia in bonum, 5
Put out into the deep, 27, 28
Thy face, Lord, do I seek, 53, 64
Ut in gratiarum semper actione maneamus, 10
Vale la pena, 119
Atonement, 16, 72, 77, 99, 110
Baptism
    gratitude for having received it, 10
    incorporation into the Church, 17
Bartimaeus, 3, 43
Beatitudes, 32, 110
Belief, 1, 9, 19, 30, 54
Bethlehem, 8, 11, 12, 115
Blessed Trinity, 31, 66, 92, 108
Holy Spirit, 2, 7, 19, 2, 27, 29, 54, 67, 70, 84, 92, 94, 108,
    116, 117
Calumny, 50, 85
Celibacy, 23
Charity
    and apostolate, 27, 92
    and fraternity, 88
    and freedom, 25
    and friendship, 35, 38

148   and good name, 50
       and heaven, 103
       and imagination, 82
       and impatience, 74
       and joy, 74
       and lukewarmness, 56
       and unity, 97
       gestures of, 28, 80
       one virtue, not two, 73
       theological virtue, 54, 112
Chastity, 23
Church
       statues in, 83
Commandments of God, 84
       of love, 24, 76, 78, 92
Communion of Saints, 6, 75, 118
Compassion, 36, 43, 63, 110
Concupiscence, 72, 94
Conversation, 7, 20, 35, 53, 61, 107
Conversion, 4, 63
Culture, 19
Death, 22, 104, 112
Detachment, 115
Discouragement, 29
Divine filiation
       and dialogue with God, 33, 61
       and fraternity, 88
       and grace, 33, 84, 108, 117
       and humility, 62, 63.
       and interior suffering, 99
       and our Lady, 108

and the Church, 17

    characteristics of, 66

    consequences of, 43, 61, 63, 84, 109

    eschatological dimension, 22

    everything is for the good

    foundation for peace and joy

    gratitude for, 10

    through Jesus Christ, 33

Duties, 61

Eternity, 64, 118

    and time, 110

Evangelization, 19, 41, 58, 96, 116

Eucharist 2, 45

    Adoro te devote, 45

    and work, 47

    souls of, 29

    institution of, 76, 77

    pledge of Heaven, 81

    real presence, 16, 40, 77

Examination of Conscience, 81, 87

Example, 19, 35, 58

    of Christ, 37, 58

    of St. Josemaría, 29

    of our Lady, 70

    of the early Christians, 96

    of parents, 97

    of Blessed Guadalupe

Faith

    and lukewarmness, 56

    and scripture, 103

    and the Cross, 106

docility, 30
in divine mercy, 55
in God, 1, 7, 18, 23, 29, 30, 33, 40, 74, 114
light of, 4, 30, 99, 112
of Elizabeth, 7
of Our Lady, 7
operative, 15
renewal of, 52

Family
and peace, 85
difficulties, 36
example to others, 5
obedience in, 24
of God, 117
of the Church, 57
role of women, 105
understanding in, 92

Family Holy, 5, 15

Fear, 4, 25, 31, 44, 71

Feasts, 64

Formation doctrinal, 57

Fortitude, 33, 105

Fraternal correction, 58

Freedom, 59, 94, 102, 114
and friendship, 35
and love, 23, 86, 114
of Christ, 59
of spirit, 7, 25, 30
our freedom, 41, 53, 59, 109

Friendship, 20, 35, 37, 38
and evangelisation, 96

and freedom, 35
authentic, 35, 36, 71
for the love of God, 19
joyous, 36, 93
of Christ, 37, 71
risky, 71
sincere, 20, 35, 37
true friendship, 20, 35, 38, 101
unique relationship, 101
with God, 20

Generosity, 3, 9
of Christ, 41
of our Lady, 20, 70

God's Love for men, 1, 10, 11, 13, 18, 30, 40, 48, 59, 76, 92, 114
and freedom, 114
and our response, 77
and work, 48
gratitude for, 10
mystery of, 11
received through Christ, 103
returning his love, 77
seen in the Gospel, 13
transforms the person, 95
very strong, 1

Good Shepherd
and guidance, 103
response in old age, 2

Gospel
reading of, 13, 41, 55, 103
shows God's love, 13

152   **Grace,** 41
    and divine filiation, 33, 84, 108, 117
    and fraternity, 88
    and interior struggle, 40
    in our Lady, 4
    in St. Josemaría, 29
    its effects and fruits, 1, 3, 28, 29, 49, 51, 53, 54, 68
Gratitude, 10
Guardian Angels, 61
Guadalupe, Blessed, 109
Heaven, 22, 106
    and definitive joy, 54
    beatitudes are the gateway, 32
Christ in, 110
    citizens of, 33
Eucharist is a token of, 81
    freedom in, 59
    help from, 68, 87
    nature of, 64
    our hope is in, 118, 119
    reason for doing things, 117
Holy Mass, 49, 76, 77, 80, 81
Holy Spirit, 25, 92, 94 116
    and freedom of spirit, 25
    at the Visitation, 7
    being open to action of, 27
    Christ is the way to, 84
    grace and power of, 54
    help to pray, 67
    our relation to, 108, 117
    participation in the Trinity, 29

    promise of, 116

    promised by Christ, 2

    strength of, 19

    teaches the Church, 116

    widening horizons, 70

    work of transformation, 233

Hope, 98

    and an apparently forced smile, 74

    and beatitude, 32

    and joy, 91

    ask Jesus for it, 54

    being filled with, 55

Cross, a symbol of, 106

    in salvific efficacy of Cross, 74

    is in heaven, 118

    lukewarmness is lack of, 56

    object of, 98

Our Lady, Mother of, 4

    true hope only with Christ, 54

Humility, 63, 69

    and humiliation, 68

God's predilection for, 7

    humility to exalt us, 68

    in the prodigal son, 62

    leads to experience joy, 32

    on the Cross, 104

    pathways to humility, 69

    practised in old age, 14

    rooted in divine filiation, 62, 63.

    vessels of clay, 119

    wretchedness and greatness, 62

154   **Illness,** 14, 16, 36, 82, 85, 104, 111

Jesus Christ, 104

and apostolate, 9

and death, 2, 39, 85, 98, 99, 104, 112

and detachment, 115

and freedom, 59

and generosity, 41

and our Lady, 4, 20, 110,

and self-giving, 51, 59, 76, 77, 81, 103, 111

and the holy women, 105, 112, 113,

as a Child, 11

availability of, 109

Blood of, 111

Calvary, 112

criticism by Pharisees, 37

crucifixion, a symbol of hope, 106

Death of, 106, 109, 110

dialogue with, 67

divine filiation in, 33

Ecce Homo, 10

fixing our eyes on, 40

following his Person, 18, 19

friendship, 36

gaze of, 43

Getsemani, 67, 99

humanity, 103

humiliated on the Cross, 104

identification with, 24, 49

immense love of, 46

in heaven, 110

in the Eucharist, 77, 80

   in the Mass, 81
   light of, 112
   loving everyone in, 37
   meeting Him, 48, 58
   mercy on us, 39
   offers us keys to heaven, 2
   on the Cross, 77
   Passion of, 39
   petitions to, 1
   prayer of, 96
   Resurrection, 7, 20, 39, 76, 105, 112, 113
   risk he takes with us, 71
   speaks to Simon Peter, 27, 0
   unity in Him, 75, 84, 118
   we show his love for humanity, 80
   we speak of Him, 35
Joy, 44, 90, 91
   at Easter, 55
   in all situations, 65, 74
   in Bethlehem, 8, 11
   in Christ, 7, 40
   in death, 22
   in doing God's will, 15
   in heaven, 54
   of friendship, 36, 93
   of mercy, 32
   of the children of God, 22, 29, 32, 33
   of the Gospel, 19, 46
   proper to Christian life, 26
   rooted in the Cross, 53, 85
   supernatural, 44

156   through evangelization, 28
Justice
    and belief, 54
    and charity, 50
    and the individual
    dealing with injustice, 1, 22, 27, 32, 82
    desire for, 94
Liturgy
    All Saints, 119
    Christmas, 8
    Corpus Christi, 45
    Easter, 7, 20, 29, 55, 76, 105, 112, 113
    Good Friday, 104, 109
Little things, 41, 47, 81
Love, 72, 89, 96, 114
    as one gets older, 14, 16
    between spouses, 16
    commandment of, 25
    dialogue of, 20
    for God, 30, 72, 76, 78, 80, 95, 98
    for Mass, 49
    for others, 48, 73, 76, 78, 83, 88
    for the Cross, 85
    growth in, 25, 53
    human love, 18, 30, 34
    lack of, 2, 56
    of friendship, 20
Lukewarmness, 56
Marriage, 23
Mass, 49, 81
    centre and root of interior life, 49, 81

consecration, 80

gospel in, 52

love for, 49

participation in, 77, 80, 81

Meekness

beatitude, 32

Mercy

and beatitude, 32

and not judging people, 94

Mercy divine, 55

and citizens of heaven, 33

and conversion, 63, 99

and Mary, 7

and the Cross, 106

and the Eucharist, 49

joy of, 32

parable of Pharisee, 68

Obedience, 24

Optimism

and beatitude, 32

and humility, 62

Our Lady

and faith in God's love for us, 92

and friendship, 20

and grace, 4, 107

and her friendships, 20

children of, 108

God's joy, 7

Holy Spirit at the Visitation. 7

life of: Annunciation, 3

life of: Bethlehem, 11, 12

158   life of: Calvary, 20, 105, 107
      life of: Cana, 20, 105
      life of: in heaven, 110
      life of: Pentecost, 116
      life of: Visitation, 20
      mediatrix, 108
      Mother of Fair Love, 92
      Mother of Hope, 4
      Spouse of the Holy Spirit, 116
      to Jesus through Mary, 52
Panama, WYD, 70
Parables of the Gospel
      Pharisee and tax collector, 68
      prodigal son, 62, 63, 64, 65
Patience, 74
      and pluralism, 102
Peace, 85, 86
      and suffering, 4, 53, 107
      and the Mass, 49
      beatitude, 32
      consequence of love, 74
      for humanity, 11
      in the family, 102
      lack of, 1
      of Christ, 12, 87, 99, 103
      sowers of, 65, 86
Penance
      and interior mortification, 87
      characteristics of, 63
      is union with Christ, 110

Persecution, 31
    beatitude, 32
    suffered by Church, 52
Pharisee, 9, 37, 40, 68
Pluralism, 102
Pope, 52, 116
Pope Benedict, 4, 25, 59
Pope Francis, 4, 19, 28, 70, 113
Poverty, 82
Prayer, 53, 61, 67, 100
    before Corpus Christi, 45
    dialogue with God, 33
    distractions in, 87
    for the Church, 52
    for the dead, 119
    is humble, 68
    notes of good, 24
    of St. Josemaría, 42, 90, 93, 119
    silence in, 1, 16
    souls of, 61, 29
    tiredness in, 100
    union with Jesus, 27, 96
    Priesthood, 80
    gratitude for, 77
    and the Mass, 80.
Rectitude of intention, 97
Sacraments
    Baptism, 17
    Confession, 5, 39, 77, 87
    Eucharist 40, 45, 76, 81, 106
    of salvation, 116

160 Shepherds at Bethlehem, 9, 11, 12, 14

St. Augustine, 27, 103,114

St. John Paul II, 59, 77, 93, 104

St. Paul VI, 19

St. Josemaría Escrivá
>   and apostolate, 19, 35
>   and creation, 41
>   and divine filiation, 88
>   and Eucharist, 98
>   and humility, 69
>   and the Blood of Christ, 111
>   aspirations of, 5, 43, 52, 53, 80, 98
>   grace in, 29
>   new year, 40
>   on birthday, 14
>   prayer of, 6, 42, 90, 93, 119,
>   youthful spirit, 29, 34

St. Joseph
>   as a father, 108
>   head of an ordinary family, 5
>   leads us to Jesus, 108
>   passage to Egypt, 15
>   peace and warmth in the home, 11, 12
>   seeking his help, 61
>   simplicity and greatness, 46

St. Mary Magdalene, 107, 112

St. Teresa of Calcutta, 119

St. Thomas Aquinas, 27, 95

Thanksgiving, Acts of, 10, 42, 67, 68, 77, 100

Unity
>   at the last Supper, 92, 96

with the Pope, 116
Virtues, 24, 32, 73, 91
Vocation, 18
    and baptism, 10
    and divine calling, 30
    and youthful spirit, 18, 34
Will of God, 24, 32, 109
Work, 47, 48
    and apostolate, 111
    and availability, 109
    and duties, 5
    and humility, 69
    and virtues, 74
    sanctification of, 6, 21, 24, 43
    seeking Jesus at, 12, 24, 28, 61, 83